My Daddy Played the Guitar

LaBreeska
Age 13

My Daddy Played The Guitar

By:
LaBreeska Rogers Hemphill

Trumpet Call Books
P.O. Box 656
Joelton, TN 37080

www.thehemphills.com
www.trumpetcallbooks.com

My Daddy Played The Guitar
ISBN: 0-9671756-8-2

Printed in the United States of America

Unless otherwise indicated, all Scripture taken from
The Holy Bible: King James Version.

Acknowledgments

~~~~~~~~~

I have lived with the idea of this book for some time now, and it finally took shape with the help of many people, to whom I am grateful.

First I want to thank my dear friends and peers Barbara Spencer and Gordon Jensen, who after reading my book *Partners In Emotion* urged me to write another. A big thanks to our secretary Dawn Mansfield who eagerly anticipated each chapter and typed them with love and devotion.

Much gratitude to my husband Joel who is a pillar of support and loves my writing. Since he is an author as well, his advice has been of utmost importance. I call him my quality control.

A big heartfelt *thank you* to Joy Mackenzie. I am honored to have such a skillful, well informed lady to do the editing and help make *My Daddy Played The Guitar* the book that it is.

A very special thanks to Lynsae Harkins of *Lynsae Design* for the cover artwork and design and to Nancy Carter of *Quality DigiPress* for the interior layout and design.

Love and gratitude to an innumerable host of family and friends whose prayers and encouragement have helped me along an interesting and exciting journey.

Table of Contents

Dedication

~~~~

In Memory Of

- Walter Erskine Rogers -

Chapter One

My Daddy Played The Guitar

My Daddy Played The Guitar

He sat beside me in the church pew, gently supporting me with his presence. My daddy, Erskine Rogers, had come to the funeral because I'd asked him to. He was seated to my left, Joel on my right. Mother's coffin was directly in front beneath a blanket of red roses.

Here I was, sandwiched between the two most important men in my life. It was a good thing, because I felt poured out like water, and it seemed that at any moment I might slip through the cracks of the wooden church floor. Oddly enough, I had never thought of my daddy as an anchor, mainly because he was not a professing Christian, as I am. I had never sat beside him in church to my knowledge, but here he was on the day that I needed him most, by my side like the Rock of Gibraltar. This was a situation that I'm sure he would have chosen to miss, but he came with dear, sweet, Lila at his side, as she had been for the past forty-four years.

The only thing linking Dad to my mother at this moment was a few faded memories of youth's new found passion. . . .and *me*.

It had all started many years ago when my daddy got his first guitar. The year was 1936 and Dad was sixteen when Papa ordered his *Stella* guitar from the mail order catalog for a whopping twelve dollars. Papa Rogers played guitar and taught his eldest son to play also. They would sit around pickin', singin', and yodelin' the popular songs of their day-mostly Jimmy Rogers tunes. (He was no relation to us.) Their music became a great pastime and provided the family and neighbors with delightful entertainment. The whole

My Daddy Played The Guitar

Rogers family knew how proud Daddy was of that guitar. Right after he got it, he was outside one day, sitting on a bail of hay, strumming along, when Hazel, his older sister came up to him with a camera.

"Erskine, I want to take a picture of you playing your new guitar," she said.

He responded by saying, "Wait, let me make sure its in tune," meaning that he would be playing when she snapped the picture, and he wanted the guitar to be in tune. To tease him, Hazel made it seem like he meant whether it was tuned or not would show up in the picture. As sisters will do, she loved to tell this on him for years to come.

My daddy and his guitar became inseparable. He spent every available hour learning all that he could about it, and his repertoire of songs continued to grow.

"All Around The Water Tank" was a favorite tune of his and Papa's, but every time Daddy sang it his baby brother Jimmy would start crying. The lyric that says; "a thousand miles away from home sleeping in the rain," painted too sad a picture for the little fellow. He just couldn't handle it.

During the time that my daddy was passionately learning to play his guitar, other things were happening on a larger scale. A new movement was making its way into parts of Northern Alabama, and causing a stir among Christians. It was labeled the "Holiness Movement." It came with thrust and landed almost in the Rogers' back door.

Those that remember the days of that revival in the late 1930's tell how it came. They describe it as *a spiritual awakening*. They said that certain Scriptures seemed to leap from the pages of the

Bible as they read them; they created a hunger for more of the Spirit and a deeper walk with God.

It was most probably a ripple effect from what was called the "Second Great Awakening" that occurred in frontier America at the turn of the previous century. When it came, it brought revival among many protestant believers.

No one person nor denomination could take credit for igniting the spiritual fire that swept through the country. It was a sovereign act of God that was occurring in many places, not just Northern Alabama.

This spiritual awakening was affecting all denominations. Many Christians had become dissatisfied with cold, formal, cut and dried church services. They wanted spirit, they wanted life, and they began to come together and seek for it. That is when revival broke out. The piney woods of Walker County, Alabama, became alive with country folk making their way to church. Some came by horseback, some by automobile, but most walked. The hills and hollows were astir. Excitement was in the air. The services started out in what was called "house church." They had separated themselves from established church buildings in order to have the freedom of worship that they desired. Eventually the crowds became so big that the services spilled out into the yard. This is how the Brush Arbor came into being.

A brush arbor was nothing more than poles driven into the ground with brush laid across the top. This was to keep the moisture out at night and provide shade from the sun during the day. They used split logs for seats, and kerosene lanterns for light. Even though creature comforts were nil, no one seemed to mind; the crowds kept coming. The atmosphere in those services was charged with hell-fire-and-brimstone preaching, public conversions, and a whole lot of heartfelt music and singing.

It was the music that drew my daddy. At those gatherings he could pick his guitar while others sang. That presented him with a great opportunity to hone his skills as a musician, and he looked forward to each service.

There were two large families that took part in supplying the music for the church that Dad attended. His family, which was the Rogers family with six children, and the Goodman family with eight. Leading those families were two mothers who had a hunger for the things of God. As time progressed, those two godly, spirit-filled ladies, were to become my precious grandmothers-Mama Rogers and Mama Goodman. From the cradle up they were my role models, my mentors and my inspiration.

The singing Goodman Family Trio was made up of my mother Gussie Mae, her older brother Howard and sister Eloise. In later years this family would become the celebrated Happy Goodman Family, known world-wide for their anointing and expertise in the Southern Gospel Music field.

During those Brush Arbor meetings and church services when the Goodmans were called to the platform to sing specials, young Erskine would join them with his guitar to help supply the music.

Mother sang alto, and my daddy played the guitar. It didn't take long for wedding bells to ring for those two. He was nineteen and she was seventeen. It looked like a marriage made in heaven. They both were young and talented and in church. But somehow it was doomed from the start. The marriage was brief. In all probability they were too young. They were both head strong; neither one would deny that. Whatever stood in the way of marital bliss took its toll twice. They divorced and remarried the second time, to no avail, and then they went their separate ways. Being their only child, I couldn't help but wonder why things turned out the way they did, but the greatest mystery of all was how my dad, after the divorce, totally separated himself from church.

Mother went on to travel and sing with her family, but Dad never did much with his talent. He seemed content to play his guitar and sing for his own pleasure. Happily I shared in both of their worlds, off and on, all of my growing up. I learned a lot from each of them that contributed to who I am and what I have become today. But their lifestyles were poles apart.

My dad liked order. He was content with "a nine to five" existence. He seldom ventured far from home, but he never stopped playing his guitar.

He played his music with such ease. It seemed to come naturally and anyone watching him could see that he enjoyed what he was doing. I loved the sound of his voice when he sang; "Rain, when are you gonna rain again rain. . . . .."

No one sounded like my daddy when it came to picking and singing. He made lovely chord progressions and pleasing tones on his guitar that enhanced his voice and the melody of the song.

It's true that my dad had talent. Often when he was playing his guitar he would take off and just pick. The "Double Eagle" was his favorite. Dad was a one-man show. He played harmonica with a wire device that clamped across his shoulders so he could strum his guitar, sing and yodel at the same time.

When he sang "Ridin' down the canyon to watch the sun go down" my childish imagination would come alive and I could picture brilliant sun-splashed cliffs under red skies. I could almost hear *"the longhorn cattle lowing*" as the cowboy went riding off into the sunset.

My daddy was an artist when it came to his music. But I will have to say that I never heard him sing a gospel song or church hymn. It baffled me how he could totally ignore religious things, especially since he was raised by a saint like Mama Rogers. As much as I loved my dad and honored him as my father, to be painfully honest, I was disappointed in him. I wanted him to be a man of God. The potential was there; he was outgoing, handsome, talented, and had everything but the main ingredient - the desire for an experience with the Lord.

From my earliest childhood I knew Dad was a sinner, and to see him saved became my lifelong quest. His lack of interest in the things of God did not keep me from loving him, and at the very core of me lay the knowledge that he was my best earthly friend. When all else failed, as long as he was on the planet, I could go to him and he would come through for me. But my daddy was lost, and that was a fact that I could hardly bear.

Living from one parent to the other and one family to the other was an education within itself. I lived two lives. Dad's surroundings were orderly and predictable, but totally without spiritual guidance. Church was not a part of his life; therefore I needed my time in his and Lila's home to be for only short intervals. I would begin to long for spiritual singing and church services, and when the opportunity presented itself, I would bundle my things together and go back to Mother. Hers was a haphazard existence because she and her brothers and sisters made their living from their musical talent. The haphazard part I never missed. It was the spiritual part that beckoned me. The Goodman's were always singing in some wonderful church or auditorium where I was exposed to many Christian influences. Because of this other world, the one that Mother and her family occupied, I knew a few things that Dad didn't know. I saw how God could take so little and do so much with it. It doesn't take a lot of capability to do something for the Lord. . . just availability.

Sitting in that little wooden church that day, with Mother's casket in full view, my grief was seasoned with hope. Her last years were spent preparing for this very occasion. Like my dad, she had tried living a life apart from the Lord for a space of time. But many years before this day, I was blessed to be in her home praying with her when she gave her heart to the Lord and found peace for her soul. Now we had brought her back home to Burnwell, Alabama to be laid to rest by the side of her parents, Mama and Papa Goodman, in the soil of those piney woods. This church itself stood as a testimony to that wonderful revival that took place so long ago. Mama Goodman's sister, Flossie, and her husband, Herschel Nix, were the founders, and their ministry could be traced all the way back to those Brush Arbor days.

Mother's salvation had been a direct answer to the prayers of mine, Mama Goodman's and many others. And it encouraged me to keep praying for my dad. I still longed for him to use his talent for the kingdom of God. For him not to do so seemed such a waste, and I just couldn't give up hope that someday he would.

If persistence pays off, then persistent I would be. So I prayed, I hoped, and I waited. . . .

Chapter Two

New Discoveries

New Discoveries

At an early age I began to distinguish the different characteristics of my two large families. I didn't know it then, but the information that my young mind was taking in was already forming the person I would later become.

From the cradle up we are making assessments about our world *and are making choices*! We are continually embracing ideas or rejecting them. A prime example of this happened before I started to school. I was spending the summer with Mother in the Goodman household. It was a warm, barefoot morning, and being an early riser I had been sauntering around in the back yard alone as the household slowly came to life.

In those days television was unheard of. We had to create our own entertainment which wasn't hard for a five-year-old like myself. So on this day it was morning in more ways than one, and I was eagerly finding new discoveries all around.

When I rounded the corner of the house, there was a disturbance on the front porch. The outburst caught my full attention, and I was drawn to it in wide-eyed wonderment. As I approached, I was surprised to find Mama Goodman in her rocking chair, nonchalantly reading the morning paper, and Bobby crying in distress. *"What is going on?"* I thought.

Bobby, my uncle, was only two years older than I, and was Mama Goodman's youngest child.

"What's wrong with Bobby?," I asked Mama Goodman. She seemed so calm in the midst of all this stir that he was causing.

"I was just reading in the paper that someone is predicting that Jesus is coming back this year," she said. At that Bobby began to jump up and down and started howling again; he was absolutely miserable. *Why would that upset him so?,* I wondered. It sounded wonderful to me. All I'd heard about heaven was nothing to be sad about. The very thought of it made me feel light and happy.

That conversation was my first awareness of the soon return of Jesus our Savior, and I embraced the news with joy. It was plain to see that Bobby was not taking it so well, and that Mama Goodman would gladly tell the news, no matter whom it upset. Let the chips fall where they may. I left that scene having made several discoveries. Namely, that Jesus is coming back, that Bobby was a sinner, and that Mama Goodman would tell it like it is, no matter if the devil himself didn't like it.

Now Mama Goodman, my maternal grandmother, was a feisty little lady that stood just over five feet tall and seemed to bark orders most of the day. She was vocal about everything. Being the mother of eight children, she was constantly trying to keep order in the house, the yard, the kitchen. She was industrious and always improving our surroundings by embroidering, quilting, gardening, canning. She had Papa making chicken coops, fences, gardens; there was activity wherever Mama Goodman was and I learned from her. She was also vocal about her Lord and her salvation. Mama Goodman had the tenacity to stand up to any Goliath in her path, and no one wondered whose side she was on.

She was a whirlwind and being the sensitive child that I was, I mostly tried to stay out of her way. But she loved me very much and doted on me. We got along well.

The Pecan Tree

Just days after the front porch episode, Bobby and I stumbled upon another discovery-a pecan tree. We wandered up to the fence that separated our back yard from our neighbor's to find that his pecan tree had a limb that came across the fence. To our delight it had dropped several tasty morsels in our yard, and we were eagerly cracking and devouring them. It was astounding to me that such wonderful nuggets could actually come from a tree! As I stood gazing up at such a phenomenon, a very angry face appeared from across the fence.

Our neighbor was shaking his fist at us and warning us to stay away from his pecan tree. They were his pecans, even those that fell on our side of the fence, and we had better not pick up another one of them! Bobby and I froze in our tracks. Then without warning, Mama Goodman came charging out of the back door like a yelping Chihuahua and giving that man a piece of her mind. "You had better leave my children alone, and anything that falls in our yard is ours!" A tirade of words ensued that could not have lasted over two or three minutes; then as abruptly as it started, it ended-with a sickening *thud*.

I heard Mama Goodman gasp and looked up to see a stream of blood trickling down the side of her face. The rock, hurled by our angry neighbor had hit just above her eye and left her dazed and in shock. Then there was silence except for an occasional sob from Mama. It was as if someone had pushed the *mute* button as Bobby and I, seemingly in slow motion, ushered my brave little grandmother back to the house. The three of us were speechless as we left the scene.

Someone called the police and we waited for them on the front porch, with Mama Goodman trembling and bleeding, to file a report.

But they never made it to our house. The patrol car stopped at our guilty neighbor's place and that is as far as they came. Nothing was ever done about the assault. Mother and the rest of the family were away in revival and Papa was unlearned in the ways of the law. Anyway, in the mid-forties in the South, the law could be biased to say the least. We came to believe that our neighbor and the police were "good ole boys" together, so that left us out.

The whole incident filled me with embarrassment and shame. I began to wonder if Mama Goodman couldn't have handled it better. But mostly I felt shame. Ashamed that I had been a witness to such ugliness, and even been the cause of it. But most of all, ashamed that a grown man was so selfish that he couldn't share a few pecans with two little dirt-poor children, and had unleashed his anger with a violent act. Harsh words weren't enough. He had assaulted my grandmother.

Becoming A Tomboy

When I stayed with Mother and all the Goodmans, I had nothing but boys to play with and became a bonafide tomboy. Bobby, being my elder, became my mentor and introduced me to the wonders of country living. We waded streams, caught "crawdads," fished, played baseball with the neighbors, and I even tried my hand with the BB gun.

The mental picture that I carry of Bobby from those times is barefoot, pant legs rolled almost to his knees, and his hair in a disorderly mass, bleached by the sun. It was told by the family, that at Bobby's birth Mama Goodman's baby sister, "Aunt Cat," came to see him. When she took her first look she moaned, "Oh I believe he's gonna have red hair and I'd rather he'd have *feathers* than red hair!" Well, it wasn't feathers, but it was red (more like auburn) and most of the time Bobby's sun-bleached hair looked like a pile of straw to me.

Bobby knew something about everything! On one of his grander hot-summer-day performances, Bobby taught me a lesson in aerodynamics. He caught a big June bug and tied a string around its leg. He then threw him into the air, and the bug took off like a kite. What a sport! We did very well with controlling the flight path of our airborne bug until he decided to land. He picked a dangerous spot on the ground beside the big red rooster. It took just one peck. The famous bug went down the hatch, and Bobby found himself with a very startled rooster at the end of his string.

Naturally since I was the only girl, there were many times as I got older that Mama Goodman counted on me when I didn't want to be counted on. Occasionally I had to hang out the wash while a big softball game was going on in plain view in the field next door. With my mind on the game, I dropped as many of the clean clothes as I hung up. Mama would make me wash them out again, adding insult to injury.

Pee Wee The Pig

One summer day it was a real scorcher. Bobby and Jimmy, my younger cousin, and I along with the kids next door, Ann and Charles Shelby, were rambling down the lane that ran alongside the Shelby's house. We were looking for something interesting and exciting to do. We followed the lane until thick woods lay on one side of us. On the other side lay Mr. Shelby's pasture.

Inside the pasture stood a barn where Peewee, Charles' blue-ribbon-winning pig lived. Charles had often assured us that Peewee was just a pet. He was Charles' 4-H project, and when he first brought Peewee home, he was so tiny that he slept in a shoe box.

27

We lingered beside the fence, and as I cautiously looked Peewee over, I wondered how that mud-covered bulk of king-sized oinks could ever be called a pet.

Without hesitation Charles topped the fence and eagerly invited us to inspect Peewee's home. We agreed and followed suit, but I kept a sharp eye on the pig. We hurried to the barn. There, Charles took several ears of dried corn and fed them to Peewee who gobbled them down like a pig! I don't know who spied Peewee's pond first or who had the bright idea that we should go for a swim in it, but all of a sudden the five of us were in full gait, headed for the water.

Bobby and Jimmy were the first in, urging the rest of us to hurry. Well, I was certainly coming, but first I had to take off my shoes and my treasured Mary Marvel watch that had been a Christmas gift just before my ninth birthday. I unbuckled the shiny blue band of the watch, placed it carefully inside one of my shoes, and away I went.

The pond was not anything like I had expected. We always swam at the creek which had a nice sandy bottom, but now mud, instead of sand, oozed between my toes and over my ankles as I waded further out. At its deepest point, the water came only to my knees, and I wondered belatedly why I hadn't noticed the soupy texture of the pond or its sickening tan color. I stood looking questioningly at my swimming hole.

Suddenly someone bellowed, "Peewee's got Breeska's watch!" I looked up in time to see the pig raise his head from my shoe, the blue strap of my watch emerging from either side of his ugly snout. I began to jump up and down screaming, "Charles do something!"

But by that time, Peewee was headed for higher ground, his back end bouncing and his curly tail bobbing up and down as he put distance between him and us. I came from the pond, almost as muddy as Peewee by this time, fists clenched and screaming wildly at Charles, "Do something! Do something!"

Charles was trying. He knew the only way to handle Peewee was with food. He ran to the barn and gathered a double handful of corn. By the time he had overtaken Peewee, the pig was happy to exchange the inedible watch for the delicious corn.

I hurried to where Peewee had dropped my watch and picked it up. It was a wreck! The crystal, the hands, and the winding stem were gone. "I hope Peewee swallowed the crystal," I hollered. "I hope it gives him a stomach ache!" I set out for home, crying bitterly, with the boys close behind.

Another surprise was in store for us when we reached the house. Mama Goodman must have been in a bad mood, because in a few minutes the three of us were taking turns dancing to the tune of a hickory switch. As she applied the limb, Mama kept saying something about us smelling like pigs and about teaching us to play in a hog wallow!

I don't suppose Peewee, the prize pig, lived to see his master, Charles, grow up, but he would certainly have been proud of him. I knew after that day that Charles had a bright, tactical mind, but what neither Peewee nor I realized was that it would lead Charles into public life and that he would someday become Mayor of Wingo, Kentucky.

The carefree attitude of Mother's family was exciting to a child like me. They'd leave for a week or two to sing and hold revivals, then come home for a week or so. This made a set routine impossible.

Sometimes they'd have a "good" trip which meant they'd come home with a little money, but often they got just enough to make it home on. They had a favorite saying that aptly describes their existence: "Chicken today and feathers tomorrow."

But those times had their pluses, and the kitchen table held the most important position in the house. Breakfast was the favorite meal. To wake up to the smell of Mama Goodman's homemade biscuits browning in the oven, fat back bacon sizzling in the big iron skillet, and the aroma of coffee perking in a much used and very worn coffee pot, was a daily happening.

There was no such thing as skipping breakfast; you were lured to the kitchen with absolutely no self-will by the mouth-watering odors and the hum of activity. All of this finished off with Mama Goodman's homemade pear preserves was more than just breakfast; it was an event. And of course not one bite was taken until we first asked the blessing over what God had so graciously provided.

Drive-In Movies, Skating Rinks and Santa Clause

Everything the Goodmans did for enjoyment, they did in a big way, making sure everyone had a good time. Sometimes we would pile into the big old nine-passenger De Soto and head for the drive-in movie to spend an evening with Abbott and Costello. As if there were not enough of us, we would invite the neighbor kids to go along. Before leaving home, we would pop loads of popcorn and put it into big grocery sacks so we would be sure to have plenty. Then off we'd go to laugh until our sides ached.

Ruth was Mother's youngest sister, and I wanted to be just like her. She and her two younger brothers, Rusty and Sam, were all in their teens together, and they were some trio. When they dressed up to go skating at night, I thought they were the prettiest people in the world. Ruth used such imagination in her selection of clothes, but it wasn't only her clothes that made her stand out in a crowd. That baby face, those dimples, and her cock-sure attitude made her an instant hit wherever she went. She was a doll and she knew it. She strutted like a four-year -old in a party dress and made you want to squeeze her.

At times Bobby, Jimmy and I, along with Mama and Papa Goodman, would get to go along to watch our three celebrities skate. What a treat! Of course when we got to the skating rink the trio stole the show by doing all kinds of fancy tricks. Ruth was so pretty every boy in the place wanted to be her partner. I remember Mama and Papa Goodman sitting contentedly on the sidelines and watching us perform.

Late one evening, Bobby and I were sauntering around the yard looking for something to do, when all of a sudden, out of the clear blue, he said "I guess you know there's not a real Santa Claus. He's your daddy." Just as calm as that! His words stung, and I felt my blood pressure begin to rise and my cheeks flush with anger. I've never been good at arguing my point, especially when I'm caught off guard. The best thing for me to do was just leave. Boy, was I mad! Bobby remained very calm and this made me angrier. I could tolerate a lot of things, but lying was not one of them, not even from Bobby. I turned on my heel and left him standing there. He could just play by himself. See how much fun that was!

I marched off, deep in thought. There was not an ounce of truth in what he said. Santa Claus *was* real. And every Christmas Eve he came right down the chimney or squeezed through the keyhole, bringing toys in a big sack. Then he filled all the stockings and hurried away, flying through the air in a sleigh pulled by eight tiny reindeer. As I thought it over carefully, I began to see a few flaws in this lovely story. I knew Santa was magic and could do anything, but how *did* he get that big sack through that tiny key-hole? It didn't make sense. For the first time in my life, I began to have doubts about that dear little man called Santa. This discovery was very painful. But one thing for sure, Bobby would never have the pleasure of knowing that he had planted a doubt in my mind!

The more mature I become, the more precious are memories from my past, like the ones I have just described. There are certain moments and occasions that click into my mind like *Kodak* still shots.

Thank God for the re-call button! It would be a terrible loss not to be able to re-visit that place in time where our society put more value on people than on things: that place of dusty roads, open windows, fires in pot-bellied stoves, kin folk dropping in to visit, and children riding bicycles and playing in the streets. My adolescent years coincided with a time when our nation was innocent, to a degree. Drug users were called dope fiends, and could be found only in far-away places, certainly not in our vicinity. Loose living was looked down upon not emulated, and locking the doors at night never crossed our minds.

I suppose there are many reasons for the straying of our nation: one is the abuse of freedom of speech. The wicked have taken this wonderful freedom and poured evil thoughts and ideas into the hearts of our children.

Not only the children, but adults have been brainwashed by the continual consumption of mental sewage from Hollywood and television. We have become dissatisfied by the glamour portrayed by plastic people in a make believe world.

My world as a child was *not* heaven. We had hardships. There were difficulties in making ends meet. There were also the age-old perplexities of differing personalities, broken relationships, and times of separation.

Despite all that, there were more positives than negatives, mostly because of my grandmothers. It mattered not with which parent I was staying, one of those dear "mamas" was always there. I also had relatives my age to play with in each household-and plenty of music. I continue to draw from those times, places, and faces stored in my memories: they stay the same, never changing in this ever-changing world.

Chapter Three

The Bayou State

The Bayou State

*I*n the early 1950's The Happy Goodmans returned home from weeks of singing all excited. And they brought with them something very interesting. They had been in Shreveport, Louisiana, and couldn't say enough about it.

Mother described how different Louisiana was from Kentucky where we lived. She told of moss hanging from the trees, and even brought a huge sample of it back for the rest of us to see. Some of the family strung it in a tree in our front yard in hopes that it would grow.

Mother said that alligators lived in the lakes and streams down there, and that big magnolia trees with huge white flowers were everywhere. I wanted to hear all about it.

What the family was most excited about was the wonderful church in which they had held a revival, Life Tabernacle. The pastor, Brother Jack Moore, was a fine man of God and had one of the largest, spirit-filled assemblies that they had ever experienced. His daughter, Anna Jean, played the grand piano like nothing they had ever seen or heard. She was extremely talented and swayed back and forth as she played. But that's not all. That wonderful church sent the family away with their needs met *financially,* which was rare. Mother and her brothers and sisters were truly blessed in the Bayou State by Pastor Jack Moore and Life Tabernacle.

I drank in all of their enthusiasm and information, never dreaming that Louisiana, that sportsman's paradise, would someday be my home-in the same decade, no less.

My Daddy Played The Guitar

By 1956 we had made several moves and were living in Evansville, Indiana when The Happy Goodman Family made a great change. Mother and all of her brothers and sisters became weary of traveling and they disbanded as a singing group. All, that is, but her oldest brother Howard, his wife Vestal, their younger brother Rusty, and me.

I was sixteen and, like the rest of the children, had started singing with the group at the first signs of talent. I don't remember it ever being discussed or decided on by vote or anything of that nature; it was just the natural thing to do. As soon as I showed interest and talent, I was taken in as part of the group. It was no big deal. I just slipped into position on stage and started singing alto along with Mother.

By the time the group decided to go their separate ways it was evident that their financial income could no longer support a family as large as ours. Everyone was forced to make a decision, find his own way and seek his own destiny. Rusty and I followed Howard and Vestal in church work. I was an "on fire" Christian and loved singing in revivals. Being in church every night fulfilled me. I loved it.

The four of us continued to travel, sing, and hold revivals, and eventually wound up in the state of Louisiana. For several months we found ourselves in and around northeast Louisiana, from one revival to another. That is how Joel and I met and began dating. Rusty was single too, and the three of us had great camaraderie going out after church to eat and doing some fishing during the day.

In 1957, the mid-March weather in Louisiana was just perfect and a far cry from what we had left behind . Our hometown of Evansville was cold and barren and still shivering under winter skies when we headed south. To find a part of the country that was lush and green with spring in full bloom and the songbirds gladly heralding its arrival was a pleasant surprise. Rusty and I readily took advantage of that. It was great to get out and soak up the warm sunshine, and fishing was the best way to do that. Joel loved it too.

I found the Bayou state to be everything that Mother had described to me and more. There seemed to be a bayou, lake, or creek, everywhere we went, and they were just loaded with crappy and brim. The three of us had a ball getting to know one another as we fished in several of those places. We not only caught fish, we saw alligators! One of the hardest things I've ever done is to wind up my pole and head for the shore with the fish still biting. We did that on more than one occasion in order to rush back and dress for church.

I'll never forget seeing my first water lilies on Cheniere lake as Joel boated us past them. I had seen only pictures of those lovely flowers before, and to actually see them and hold one in my hand gave me the feeling of stepping out of a page of a story book.

Then there was the grey moss that adorned the cypress trees and hung like costly lace all around us, swaying gently in the breeze. It was truly a different world. Every now and then I'd catch a whiff of honeysuckles or the sweet smell of Cape jasmine growing in the wild. All of those scenes and fragrances toyed with my emotions and made a perfect setting for love to grow. And grow it did!

When Joel proposed marriage we were both seventeen. (He lacked two months being eighteen). But I had found the place where I wanted to live for the rest of my life, and I had found this wonderful Christian young man to share it with. The place I'm talking about was a little burg on the outskirts of West Monroe, called Bawcomville. It was out past the paper mill and across the levee.

Nothing about this tiny community would entice the average outsider to want to put down roots there. The smell of the paper mill was a constant and made me gag and hold my nose every time I passed it.

Urban Renewal certainly hadn't found this location. To put it mildly, this was a poor settlement in every way but one. That was the site of Joel's home church, where his Dad and Mom pastored and where he played guitar in the church band.

Howard, Vestal, Rusty, and I had held two revivals in that lively, thriving, Full Gospel church in the past several months, and it was inspiring. Also to watch Joel play his guitar along with the rest of the musicians, to me seemed providential. This is the way it had been with my mother and dad many years before.

Dad Hemphill had gathered his congregation from all walks of life and poured them full of the Word of God, along with love and acceptance. The Holy Spirit was evident in their music and worship, and I loved that church from the moment I first entered its doors.

Mom and Dad Hemphill, their family, and the church family gave me the courage to say *"yes"* to Joel's proposal. That meant leaving my family, friends, and familiar surroundings, and it was a big leap of faith for someone as young as I was.

Joel and I were crazy about each other, and love was new and grand. But I'm not so sure that I would have had the courage to make such a decision if all the above ingredients had not been in place. However they were, and when Joel popped the question, my immediate response was, "That paper mill sure does smell good!"

Our wedding was plain and simple without many of the usual trimmings. When the Goodmans left for parts unknown to hold another revival and left me standing in the yard, I waved them happily on. I was looking forward to my new role in life in my new surroundings.

Then came the rain, torrents of it! It rained and rained *and rained* in the summer of 1957. The sun hardly showed its face for six long miserable weeks, and for the first time I began to have doubts. Joel went to work every day, painting with his brother Dan, and I was going stir-crazy looking at the walls. It was then that I had second thoughts about my decision to live in Louisiana. Of course, it goes without saying that before long, the sun came shining through-in more ways than one.

Old Green Eyes

The following year found me great with child, the thing I wanted most. I had even cried once after several months of marriage when I realized I was not expecting. Joel and I were eager to begin our family. We were just kids ourselves but we knew what we wanted. We wanted each other, we wanted children, and we wanted to work for the Lord. These things we did as we ventured into life, full steam ahead, savoring every moment of it. Well, not every moment. As in every young marriage, there were things at the very beginning that had to be worked out.

The first hurdle we had to overcome was a big one. Jealousy! With love comes the desire to possess (which is impossible to achieve) and brings on an abundance of problems. The old green-eyed monster moved in with Joel and me for about the space of two years. His first attack was on Joel.

I was outgoing, had traveled over a big part of our nation, and was very mature for my years. Or so it seemed. Joel, on the other hand, was a small-town boy, private and shy by nature, and felt overshadowed by my ability to mix and mingle. This was a prescription for real problems, and they came. But Joel had enough spiritual training to take his problem to church. He received counseling, prayer, and help before I ever knew there was a problem.

My experience was much more complicated. When my body began to change with our first pregnancy, I changed too. I became insecure, emotional and extremely jealous.

I can see where a marriage can be stymied at this crucial point, and never recover, because I came to the precipice.

No wonder Solomon said, "Jealousy is as cruel as the grave." I can attest to the fact that it is a living hell, and it doesn't have to make sense. I became jealous over the most bizarre, foolish things: family, friends, job, even Joel's good looks.

That old monster told me that Joel would have been better off if he had married someone else; that I was not his equal.

Jealousy isn't loveable, but it demands love in a very ugly way, causing love to diminish and just dry up. Our marriage was in trouble!

At one point I talked to my mother about my problem. She admitted that when she and Dad were married, she was jealous of his guitar. She said she had wanted him to spend that time with her, not the guitar. That helped me understand that my problem was not an isolated one. But I also came to understand that I was the only one who could change my disposition. It became evident that the survival of our marriage now hinged on my willingness to come to my senses and *let it go.*

One night just after one of my tantrums, Joel and I went to bed in silence. We were both worn thin from my fabricated jealousies. Love was waning. It had no room to grow. My accusations and tears were causing us both to dry up inside, wishing we were someplace else.

That night became the moment of truth for me. Fear gripped my heart. I was losing Joel over nothing, and driving him away from me instead of drawing him closer.

It's as if scales fell from my eyes, and the ugly picture of our sad state loomed before me. All of a sudden I realized how tired I was of crying. I wanted to laugh and be happy again. I wanted to be teased and loved by that happy, gentle, God-fearing husband that I had married. The ball was in my court!

The chilling silence was broken that night with this declaration. "Joel, from this moment on I will never be jealous of you again, but I can't do it by myself. You'll have to help me! Tomorrow will be different. You'll see." With those words we received some degree of comfort and rolled over and fell asleep.

The following day *was* different because I had made up my mind to change, and I did! It may sound too simple to work, but it does. That green-eyed monster had to move on; I was sick and tired of his miserable lies.

A load lifted from both of us, and in no time we were laughing, loving and building a life together because I devised a plan and stuck to it. I swallowed my pride for the sake of my marriage and admitted that I had been wrong and was willing to change.

I am convinced today, as I was then, that if I hadn't faced reality and taken my part of responsibility in our problems, our marriage would not have lasted. Joel helped by being more careful to include me in his decisions and discussions. He made me feel more a part of things rather than just a newcomer. I no longer felt that I was taken for granted, and our marriage soon became planted on firm ground.

Chapter Four

Bastrop

Bastrop

The eager congregation wouldn't take "no" for an answer. They wanted to hear a song by their new pastor and his wife. The more I protested, the more they clapped and cheered. They were determined, and I still can't believe I did it! The date was June 9, 1961 at a Friday night youth rally. This was our first service since we were voted in as pastor of the little interdenominational church in Bastrop, Louisiana.

Not wanting to start off on the wrong foot, I reluctantly made my way to the platform to join Joel and give them what they wanted. We sang.

The following morning, June 10, found me in the hospital giving birth to our third and final child, Candy. At the ripe old age of twenty-one, Joel and I were the parents of three children and pastoring a little country church. Bastrop was about thirty miles from Bawcomville and Mom and Dad Hemphill. As far as I was concerned, it just didn't get any better than that. Joel and I had our hands full with our little family and the church family, but I was definitely in my element.

Bastrop was a great place to raise children. It was a small paper mill town, boasting about twelve thousand in population. When I say paper mill town that is for sure what I mean, it had *two* paper mills. The Lord is bound to have a sense of humor. He took me up on it when I told Joel, "That paper mill sure smells good," and gave me two! To be honest it *didn't*. Sometimes it smelled more like rotten cabbage, but you kind of get used to it. Actually those who relied on the paper mill for a living said it smelled like ham and eggs to them. Since many of our congregation worked for the mill, I was inclined to agree.

Stepping On My Toes

Mine and Joel's work for the Lord seemed insignificant in comparison to what was taking place across the nation. Those were the days of the Kennedys-the razzle-dazzle days that came to be known as Camelot. You couldn't go anywhere without seeing their pictures splashed over the newsstands. Television, newspapers, and every leading magazine was having a heyday with this enormous, glamorous family. They took our nation by storm!

One day Joel came in with the newspaper and a picture of someone dressed in a ski uniform. You couldn't even tell if it was a man or woman, let alone recognize who it was. The skier was completely camouflaged behind cap, goggles, and scarves. Joel had the caption folded underneath the picture and said, "I'll give you a dollar if you can tell me who this is." If I'd been smart I would have made him bring it up to ten, because I knew exactly who it was. Jackie couldn't go anywhere without the whole nation knowing, and I had heard on the news the previous day that she was headed for the ski slopes. I got the dollar!

If you balanced our lives on a scale with the Kennedy's, we wouldn't weigh even as much as a grain of sand. But I can truthfully say that I wouldn't have traded places with Jackie in all of her glory. Their jet-set lifestyle had no appeal to me. I was fulfilled, and we were making a difference in the lives of those who sat under Joel's teaching and came under the influence of the Word of God.

I will have to say however that when Bobby and Ethel kept having children, I felt a twinge of envy, thinking how nice it would be to be able to afford to have all the children you wanted. When I was a young girl and my friends were dreaming of becoming nurses, airplane stewardesses, school teachers, etc., all I ever wanted was to have my own Christian family. What greater contribution could I make to the world than present it with my most valued possessions, my children?

Raising a family was a role I took seriously. For the first few years it took all the patience and wisdom I could muster to be a fair referee and administer the right amount of discipline, mixed with love, to produce offspring that I could be proud of. I couldn't do it alone, and thank the Lord I didn't have to. Joel was an attentive and doting father. The Holy Spirit also guided me when I went to the Lord in prayer. Many times behind the closed doors of my bedroom in prayer, I received strength and wisdom to accomplish the monumental task set before me. At one point I remembered the words of Mom Hemphill: "Today they are stepping on your toes; tomorrow they'll step on your heart."

Well, I knew nothing about my little ones stepping on my heart, but I sure knew about them stepping on my toes.

One day Joel and I walked into the house from the front yard. We could hear a lot of giggling, so we followed our ears to the kitchen to see what was so funny. There they were, all three of them, on their knees in front of my dining room chairs. One of them had found the ice pick and they were taking turns punching holes in the plastic chair bottoms-just to hear the *poof* of escaping air. Every time it *poofed* they let out a giggle. They were having a blast! When their daddy and I appeared in the doorway, it caught them by surprise. All three of them looked up at us as guilty as "the cat that ate the canary" with the tail feathers still protruding.

"What are you doing?!" I asked in exasperation. Then with a sinking heart I moaned, "You just can't have anything with kids!!"

I realize that plastic-covered dinette chairs do not sound like much to lose, but they were all I had, with no prospects of being able to replace them. So for the next two years, as long as we lived in the parsonage, we had *perforated* dinette chairs for our many guest to enjoy, as they sat at our table for a meal.

Raising three small children was a challenge and was never boring. Like the time five-year-old Candy hid in the back seat of the car to go with Joel as he went to preach a funeral. He was in a hurry (about to be late) but needed to stop at the service station because the gas gauge was showing empty. Joel got out of the car while the attendant was pumping the fuel and just happened to glance in the back window. There lay Candy, sweaty, barefoot and in old play clothes. When she saw that he had spied her, she jumped up giggling, real pleased with herself, and said "I fooled you didn't I Daddy?" With no time to spare, all he could do was take her into the restroom and try to wash her up. Then he called me and said, "Honey, Candy is with me. I'm taking her to the funeral."

"Why, didn't you tell me you were taking her with you? I've been frantic looking for her! Besides, she's not dressed and looks like a ragamuffin!" I exclaimed

"I didn't know it," he said. "She hid in the back seat and I found her when I stopped for gas at the service station. I don't have time to bring her home. There is nothing left to do but take her with me." It was an embarrassing situation, knowing that there would be a lot of raised eyebrows and whispered questions as to how that preacher's wife could "send her little girl with her daddy to a funeral looking like that!"

Making My World Better

There is an old adage that says "You can't see the forest for the trees." I'm afraid that was a description of me. I became so immersed in child rearing and homemaking that sometimes the big picture escaped me. My nose stayed to the grind with "at the moment" happenings. Washing, cooking, refereeing, rushing to dress my children and myself for church, and a host of unforeseeable crises in between. I was on a treadmill with no immediate relief in sight. It's understandable that a young mother of three small children can get bogged down and irritable at times. The simple things that we take for granted such as sitting down to a quiet meal, or going to bed with a favorite book, or just having a decent conversation with a friend or your husband without chaotic interruptions were things long gone. With all this in mind, Joel and I devised a plan. We decided to take one night a week for ourselves. It didn't have to be big or costly - just a night out for a meal and some time alone.

On one such occasion the two of us were at a little hole-in-the-wall restaurant in downtown Bastrop and had enjoyed a leisurely meal. When Joel went to the cash register to pay the bill, I wandered over to a stack of pamphlets along the wall, picked up one and stuck it in my purse. To pick up a pamphlet as though I had time to read it was odd for me. Usually I fell into bed every night totally exhausted. About the only thing I took time to read at short intervals was my Sunday School lesson.

All was quiet when we returned home that night. The children were snuggly tucked in bed by the sitters, and sound asleep. This was a luxury that I wasn't used to, so I reached for the pamphlet, crawled into bed beside Joel, who was lying there enjoying his newspaper, and began to read. What I read revolutionized my life.

The little pamphlet titled, *"A Better World Begins With **Me**,"* was telling me how to make *my* world a better place to live in-by scattering love and sunshine, beginning with my husband and children.

In essence the author, Becky Burris, was urging me to stop waiting on others to *give* to me, and *start dishing out*. She challenged her readers to give to families, friends and others the very things that they would like to receive from them. She pointed out that if we want a pat on the back for a job well done, to look around and do the same for someone else.

If we enjoy a sincere compliment on the way we look, or for a deed we have done, *give one* to someone who deserves it. There isn't a parent in the world who doesn't like to have his child put his arm around him and say, "I love you." There isn't a husband or wife who doesn't like to hear that he or she is appreciated and loved. Yet it seems everyone is waiting on someone else to make the first move.

When I turned out the light, I knew that *my* world was about to change for the better! *I* was going to change it. The next morning found me up earlier than usual with eager anticipation. I had found a key to unlock the love that is in my heart by putting it into action. It was also the key to a better, happier attitude.

There was not going to be any more time for petty feelings of being slighted. I would be too busy paying attention to those around me and making their world better-with a smile, a kind word, and more affection!

There is no way to describe the influence that this pamphlet has had on shaping my life. It set me on a path that reaps mega rewards. From that day forward I have made it a habit to give the kind of sincere treatment that I like to receive. It sure makes life sweeter, and like "bread on the water" it just keeps coming back!

That's not to say that my many chores of motherhood let up; that didn't change. But I changed. I taught myself to look around and see what was important, what was lasting, and what my family and friends needed most from me. I found that everyone needs love, understanding, forgiveness from time to time, and kindness. And it doesn't cost a thing!

The Assassination

My Mother lived in Dallas and had a great job sewing for the company that created the *Prophecy* clothing line. The building where she worked was across the street from the Texas Schoolbook Depository, that infamous building where Lee Harvey Oswald hid on the fateful day of November 22, 1963. The gunshots that resounded around the world, taking the life of our young president and piercing the hearts of millions, were actually heard by Mother and Aunt Stella.

As they sat at their sewing machines that day, the big windows were open to a breeze and the festive sounds of the parade passing by on the street below. Mother couldn't see what was happening, but when she heard the gunshots she gasped, "They have shot our president!" At that moment, in Bastrop, Joel and I and our children were sitting at the table having lunch. The telephone rang in the hall, and Joel got up to answer it. A young man from our church said, "Brother Joel, President Kennedy has just been shot!"

That assassin's bullet rocked our world with the death of our

President and left in its wake an unsteadiness in our nation that lingers today.

Christmas

Every year for Christmas, Mother was so sweet to give us something to make our lives a little better. That Christmas, since we needed living room furniture, she sent a check, and we bought a wine-colored, naugahyde sofa, and matching swivel chair. It wasn't much to boast about, but we were happy to have it.

When you start off with nothing, everything that you accumulate has a much greater value than its actual worth. What goes into the evaluation of a certain article is how long it took to get it, and what it would take to replace it. Joel and I started out with nothing. The furniture that we had gathered wasn't much to brag about, but it was ours and we were pleased.

The children and I loved Christmas time, and were excited about putting up the first tree in our new home. Spirits were high as the kids left with their dad that evening to find the perfect tree. I was fixing supper when they arrived and stood the big cedar in our living room. The decorations were taken from storage and strewn all over the floor. Nine-year-old Trent busied himself by sitting down on the new sofa and trying to sort out the tree lights. They were the ones with big bulbs, handed down to us from Grandma Hemphill.

Ever so often he would plug them up to check his progress and count how many bulbs he was going to have to replace. Those were the things that were merrily taking place when I called the gang to supper. Everyone gulped down their food, anxious to get back to decorating our lovely tree. When we returned to the living room, we smelled something burning. You guessed it! The Christmas lights were left on, and everywhere a bulb was touching the sofa it left its imprint burned into the naugahyde. Poor Trent. It made him sick. We all were. It was an honest mistake, one that any of us could have made, so we didn't scold him. He already felt bad enough. But that sofa with the burned spots graced our living room for years. Much later when we moved to Nashville, it was loaded up with the rest of our possessions and came along with us to the big city.

The piano was a different story. Candy loved candles, and added to our decorations that year by making a lovely arrangement for our black, baby grand piano. She tore remnants from cedar limbs left from the tree, made a circle, set a big candle into the middle of it, and set it on the piano. The whole family applauded her creative genius. For an eight-year-old she could come up with some great ideas, and this seemed to be one of them.

The piano was one that we had given someone fifty dollars for because it had a busted block, and would no longer hold a tune. But we played it anyway, and it made a lovely piece of furniture, giving the appearance of affluence. We were proud of that piano!

When we left the house one evening to go Christmas shopping, we turned on the tree lights to be seen through our big picture window. Without our knowledge, Candy went back into the living room and proudly lit her candle. When we returned hours later we were blessed to have a home to come back to. The candle had burned down through the cedar, and had created a big hole in the piano. It was still smoking with live coals when we walked in, but somehow the wood was slow burning; otherwise we would have come back to ashes, never knowing the cause. The Lord was gracious to us that year. If it hadn't been for Him, such stories might have had a tragic ending. Instead they are happy memories of a time when a struggling little couple was busy making a life, a good life. It was a time when our children were around our feet, stepping on our toes, but it didn't hurt.

It seems ludicrous to make mention of how little we had monetarily back then, because *things*, great or small, don't produce the "warm fuzzies" when you reflect on them. It is the fascinating acts of living, surrounded by those who mean all the world to you, that you remember and value. Therefore Joel and LaBreeska Hemphill were very rich indeed. We know it *now*, but we also knew it *then*.

Chapter Five

Alla Mae and Cobby

Alla Mae and Cobby

"*B*rother Joel, come quickly. . . .Bobby Ray has been shot!"

The frantic call came from the home of Alla Mae and Cosby White. It was Wednesday and we were getting ready for the evening service. Bobby Ray Hammond had recently married into the White family, one of the largest families in our church. Even though he came regularly with his wife Barbara and his in-laws, he had not made a commitment to serve the Lord on his own.

He had sat through some powerful services, especially the one last Sunday night. Though Joel had his sermon prepared, we didn't get past the praise and worship. The service flowed in another direction with lots of music, singing, testimonies and altar call. It was wonderful. We were amazed that anyone could sit through all that without giving his heart to the Lord. But Bobby Ray never made a move.

After the phone call, Joel rushed to the home of the White's, arriving just before Barbara. She soon came in from the hospital emergency room, grief stricken and in shock. Bobby Ray was dead.

When Barbara saw her pastor she fell on his shoulder. "Brother Joel, it wouldn't be so hard, but I know he's in hell right now" she gasped between sobs.

Today, forty years later, the memory of that statement still brings tears to Joel's eyes. Of course we are not permitted to make such judgements because he, along with all departed people, are in the hands of a just and merciful God.

Barbara eventually regained her composure, and the horrific story unfolded as she haltingly, and tearfully, described what had happened.

She and Bobby Ray had loaded up several of the kids, cousins, nieces and nephews into the old pickup truck. It was a hot summer day and they were headed for the creek on the back side of the pasture for a quick swim. Then they were going back to the house to dress for church. This was something they did often. . . .to help the kids get cleaned up all at once.

Bobby Ray had grabbed the 22 caliber rifle, and stood it on the floor between him and Barbara. He was planning to shoot some turtles, and possibly a snake, while the children swam.

The truck had to first go through the pasture gate, and one of the boys jumped out of the back to open it, then chained it behind them. As they bounced along, they came to a curve in the dirt road. When Bobby Ray turned the wheel, the gun, known to have a hair trigger, slid toward him and went off. His hand was on the steering wheel, and the bullet went through his wrist and straight into his heart. The truck lurched to a stop, and Barbara managed to push him over and get under the wheel. The children jumped out of the truck, and Barbara took off driving wildly for the hospital. She crashed through the gate, and just a half mile from the hospital the old farm truck ran out of gas.

Barbara was sitting there screaming hysterically, her husband lying in the seat beside her, bleeding and unconscious, when the policeman found them. They rushed Bobby onto the hospital, but he was dead on arrival. The doctor said that there was nothing that he could have done for Bobby, even if he'd been standing right there when the gun went off. We called off service that night because everyone connected was in shock. It was such a tragedy and so unexpected.

God is sovereign. No one knew that Bobby's time on earth would be cut so short. And certainly no one can say where he is today. When he was desperate for a job a few weeks before, the White family asked the church to pray about it, and in no time, he landed a good job and was so thankful that he paid his tithe that first week. So I certainly would not judge him and would love to know that he was welcomed home to heaven. But when Joel showed me the title of his Sunday night sermon - the one that he never got to deliver - I shuddered. It was titled, *""Can thine **heart** endure, or can thine **hands** be strong, in the days that I shall deal with thee? I the Lord have spoken it . . . ." (Ezekiel 22:14).*

Brother and Sister White were faithful members of our church and they were a delight. His name was Cosby but she called him "Cobby" and he called her "Alla Mae." They were up in years when they gave their hearts to the Lord, and Joel baptized them.

Brother White, a retired paper mill worker, had been known for his boisterous way and use of profanity. So the change that came about when he got saved was a strong witness to the entire community.

He had a prominent scar on his forehead from an old injury that caused him to have severe headaches. The Lord took care of that too. He was healed one night in church and the headaches disappeared. When he told about the Lord healing him, he had a country way of expressing himself. He'd say "I use to take aspirin like a chicken eatin' corn before I was healed, but not anymore."

Brother White loved his church and his pastor. All Joel had to do was hint that something needed to be done around the church or parsonage, and he would show up the next day dressed in overalls, with his tools, ready to work.

In describing this dear man I need to add that he wore glasses tied on with a piece of elastic. I assumed that this was a safety precaution that he took while working in the mill to keep from losing them, but it became a part of his make up. It mattered not how dressed up he was - suit and tie, the whole works - you could always count on that piece of elastic tied in a knot at the back of his head. Brother White was also tough. Joel would smile whimsically at times when they were working together and the old gentlemen would use the small blade of his pocket knife, (hopefully dull) to clean out his ears. Joel had cringed in times past at older men using their keys for this purpose, but a *knife blade* was a first.

Sister White was just a large lovable mama, and like many women from her era, humbly deferred to her husband. They lived several miles from town in a rambling country home without many trappings. They were just plain and simple and had raised a very large family. Joel and I loved to go there.

Brother and Sister White had thriving gardens with all kinds of fresh vegetables. They had various livestock, including a duck pond full of ducks. When we had out of town guests, usually preachers or singers, we took them to the White's farm to ride horses. We even took my uncle Rusty Goodman and his wife Billie.

The Whites took us in as their own. Many Sunday's after service would find Joel and me and our children having dinner with them. Most of their children were grown and married with their own families, but it was not uncommon for all of them to be there for "Sunday dinner." When we arrived, the women would be busy in the kitchen putting the finishing touches on the turkey and dressing or duck and dressing, to be served with potato salad and loads of all kinds of country food. On these occasions there was an abundance of everything including *people*. The men would gather on the big front porch in swings and rocking chairs, laughing and exchanging hunting tales, while the children ran and played in the yard. The White's home was definitely the happening place to be for a Sunday meal!

When it came time to eat they had a custom that I found interesting and never quite got use to. All of the White family, adults and kids alike, would gather and wait for Joel to pray over the food, then leave for the living room or other parts of the house so their Mother and Dad could enjoy a quiet meal with Joel and me.

Then after we left the table, the rest of the family migrated toward the kitchen to fix their own plates. I always felt uncomfortable with this set up and tried to finish my meal as soon as I could without appearing to rush Brother and Sister White.

One day Brother White showed up at our house dressed in overalls. He had two Mimosa trees in the back of his pick-up. It bothered him that we didn't have enough shade in our back yard. He called them "Moppa" trees and said that they were fast growing; then he proceeded to dig holes and plant them.

The Mimosa trees did grow swiftly, and in no time they provided us with a nice shade, covered with lovely pink blossoms. That was many years ago and "Cobby" and "Alla Mae" have long been gone from our midst, but not the precious memories that they left behind. The huge "Moppa" trees are still standing as a reminder of that dear couple who graced our lives with their caring and their sharing.

My Daddy Played The Guitar

Prayer:
Thank you Lord for the good people I have known and loved. And thank you that good-bye down here doesn't have to be forever. Amen.

Chapter Six

The Baptizing

The Baptizing

My stocking feet suddenly left the ground, and I landed with a big splash in the creek-on my posterior! It was a very undignified landing, with arms flailing, feet in the air, and dressed in my Sunday-go-to-meeting clothes. While bobbing up and down, sputtering, and trying to keep my head above the water, I couldn't believe what had happened.

It was Sunday around noon. Joel had dismissed the morning service earlier than usual for a baptizing. These were special events that took place out in the country at what was commonly known as the cave-off. This beautiful flowing creek with sandy banks and bottom was a favorite swimming hole of ours also. It was where we took our children to swim in the summer months, as did many of our neighbors and friends.

As usual, several of the church members took their cars, and in a caravan, we left without even going home for lunch. There were many new converts to be baptized including Cosby and Alla Mae White, but it wouldn't take long, and it was an occasion that I always looked forward to.

After everyone arrived and gathered on the bank, Joel waded out into the water about waist deep. He had some sort of staff that he carried with him to make sure of the depth, and to stick up in the bottom of the creek, as a hanger for the towel that was slung about his neck. I was proud of him. He did it the way his father before him did, and it was so official. He would then lead those of us gathered on the bank in a couple of hymns while he stood in the water with hands raised toward heaven. This never failed to bring tears to my eyes. It moved me deep down inside. We were carrying out a commission that had been a part of Christianity since the beginning of the church age and I felt connected. *When We All Get To Heaven* and *In The Sweet By and By* were favorites at those services, and I knew that this was part of the process that would take us there. After the singing, all of those to be baptized held hands and waded out, with the help of some of the brethren, to where Joel was standing. He would then take them, one a time, and have them kneel in the water. This made it easier for Joel to handle each person, large or small. After saying the necessary things over them, he gently buried them in the water in the name of Jesus our Lord.

That particular day was a scorcher. My dress was sticking to me as the sweat trickled down my back. In the early sixties it was unheard of to go to church without hose, high heels, and all of the undergarments that went with being "gussied up." I had already stepped out of my shoes, and was standing close by, when Joel came out of the water. We stood there together, and in my misery, all I could think of was that beautiful, refreshing stream. I leaned over to Joel and jokingly said "I wish someone would push me in." The words were still in my mouth when I became airborne! *He* pushed me in!!

While I was still trying to gain my composure-and balance-others started joining me. The young people were jumping in right and left. They reasoned that if the preacher's wife could go swimming in dress clothes, they could too!

The Parsonage Bathroom

Youth is a wonderful thing; its fun loving, innocent, and for the most part, fearless. I sure had fun growing up as a pastor's wife and

I wouldn't trade those memories for anything. I need to add right here that a baptismal tank was out of the question at our little country church. We didn't even have running water.

There was an old outside privy that stood to the left of the sanctuary, out in the "boonies." Joel tore it down immediately after becoming pastor. We then left the door of the parsonage, which was close by, unlocked, and let the folks have access to our bathroom. This made more sense to Joel and me than the alternative. Somehow it never occurred to us that this was an inconvenience.

I thought that since *we* were public property, everything that we had was also. Having the public going in and out of our house just wasn't a problem. I can truthfully say it never bothered me. When you don't have much, you don't have much to lose. We certainly didn't have anything worth stealing, but that wasn't part of my thinking in those days. I thought I was rich. I had everything I ever wanted, and I was truly happy and savoring each day and each new experience.

That is not to say that we didn't hit a few rough spots along the way. For instance, someone brought it to my attention, that when they went to the parsonage to use our bathroom, they happened upon a couple sitting in the dark on our living room sofa, hugging and kissing.

I hated to have to pass the news along to Joel, but eventually I had to tell him that a couple had been found "necking" on our living room sofa.

He went ballistic! I couldn't believe he was taking it so hard. Stealing a kiss now and then was all a part of being a teenager. And we sure had a lot of youth at our church. I taught the teens and had as many as fifty on any given Sunday. Joel just wasn't taking this news about the couple very good. Then I heard him recounting it to one of the church elders, and he said "someone found a couple *naked* on our sofa!" I stopped him. "No, no!" I said, "They were *necking*!" I sure was glad to find out what he thought I said before the next service, because he would have "let the hammer down," and there would have been a big uproar over the naked couple that never was!

Then there was the time that a sister in our church, who was the mother of a large family, had an urgent call of nature. When she went to the parsonage she found the bathroom door locked and banged on it to no avail. Finally one of her children came running into the church, found Joel, and told him of the dilemma. By the time he got there our dear sister was wringing her hands, walking the floor, and praying. Someone must have locked the door and pulled it to, there was just no way to get in. Joel moved fast! There was an outside bathroom window. It was painted white for privacy. Joel ran, got a chair, pulled it up to the window, and raised it. To his great surprise there sat five-year-old Trent, bewildered by all the commotion, and embarrassed. Trent looked up at Joel and meekly said, "Hi Dad!" Joel immediately sized up the situation and realized what had happened. Trent was very private, and he thought if he didn't say anything, they would go away and come back later. He had no idea that it would turn into a full-scale fiasco.

Moved with compassion, Joel asked tenderly, "Are you all right Son?"

"Yes Sir" Trent replied.

Then his Dad said, "Son if you are through, go ahead and open the door. Someone else needs to get in."

With that, Trent quickly opened the door, and took off for higher ground.

The "bathroom in the parsonage" episode soon became nothing more than a few whimsical memories as our assembly continued to grow and flourish. It wasn't long before we were breaking ground for the new sanctuary with all the modern conveniences.

Chapter Seven

Hitting The Nail On The Head

Hitting The Nail On The Head

*J*ust about every church deals with one. If not now, then somewhere in the near future-there seems to be plenty to go around. I'm talking about a member who had rather *lead* than *follow*. Ours was Sister Pierce[1].

When Sister Pierce came to church, she entered the sanctuary flanked by her married daughters and their children, much like Mother Superior and her underlings. She was a good woman and could be a blessing to most any pastor. In fact she had been a blessing to *many* pastors. Somehow she couldn't "stay put" at a church for very long. Now she had come our way to check Joel and me out. We were new in town and very young.

I think that must have appealed to her motherly instincts. It didn't take long to find out that Sister Pierce excelled in "taking charge" - like seeing the need for a church yard cleaning, or planting shrubs and flowers on the grounds. Or if someone died anywhere in town, it mattered not if any of us knew them, Sister Pierce did; so she felt it her duty to rally the troops to help the bereaved. Now all of this was well and good, but she would do this by interrupting service at any time she pleased. She would stand up at the most inopportune time, state the need, then call for volunteers. She would then proceed further by delegating certain women to cook certain dishes for certain days. Now this disruption had a way of going on and on. But the sheer pleasure that showed in her face could not be mistaken. She was in the driver's seat, right where she belonged,

---

[1] Not her real name.

and it felt good. Sister Pierce didn't take into account the fact that Joel was not a novice when it came to pastoral savvy, even though he was young. When it came to understanding the motives and actions of his church members, he usually saw it for what it was worth, having been raised in a pastor's home. Joel had just about seen it all, but he was very patient with her.

One morning Joel picked up the phone to give Sister Pierce a pastoral call, just a friendly chat to see how she was doing. Now in those days, when you made a phone call, you actually talked to the operator and gave her the number; she would then connect you with the desired party. Somehow the operator mistakenly patched him in on a conversation already in progress. Sister Pierce was on the line to another lady in our church airing her grievances. "Brother Joel," it seems, was the topic of the conversation. She was plainly agitated because he wasn't running things to suit her. Now Joel didn't mean to eavesdrop but couldn't help what he had overheard. So he hung up the receiver with a smile, without saying a word. They never knew.

His sermon the following church night was about gossiping on the telephone. He admonished his flock to be careful about sowing discord by running down the pastor and the church. He wound up by asking our church family to promise the Lord, and their pastor, that they would not get on the phone and talk negatively about the church or its members. Then he asked for a show of hands to seal their commitment. Hands were raised all over the sanctuary. Gossip seems to be a small-town problem and ours was no exception.

One day on Joel's rounds to visit his parishioners, he found himself in Sister Pierce's neighborhood and decided to stop by. When he knocked on the door, Mr. Pierce was the one who opened it. Joel was shocked to find the old gentlemen red faced - and visibly angry when he saw who was at the door. Mr. Pierce was not a professing Christian and had never been to our church, but it seems that he had heard all about it, and what he heard wasn't good. The moment he saw Joel he was ready to fight!

He raised his voice in anger and said "I'm seventy-two years old, but I'm not too old to scrap." Joel couldn't believe his ears and came back with, "Mr. Pierce, I am twenty-five years old and I am too old to scrap." With that he excused himself and left.

I don't know if it was the continued upheaval in his home, or just declining health, but in less than six months Joel was called on to preach Mr. Pierce's funeral. On his sick bed, just before his passing, he let Joel know that he was sorry for that confrontation, and restitution was made.

Joel then took the opportunity to talk to him about his soul. At that point Mr. Pierce was very weak, but he tearfully expressed belief in the Lord, and Joel felt hopeful about his salvation.

I suppose that Sister Pierce remained a member of our church as long or longer than she had any other church in town. But the inevitable finally happened. She left. She had so many good qualities but could never quite grasp the basic rule of leadership, that in order to lead you must first learn to follow. It was in the dead of winter when she made up her mind to go. And she began to gather up the things she had donated, including the one and only space heater in the living room of the parsonage. It was extremely cold the day they came for it. I couldn't believe what was happening. In dismay, my children and I watched as they disconnected our only source of heat and went out the door with it!

Somehow we survived that ordeal without harm except for our spirits.

One day the following spring, Joel was on top of the new church building with several of the men, nailing on shingles. Someone brought up Sister Pierce's name in the conversation, and our last episode with her was still fresh in Joel's mind.

"Let me tell you about Sister Pierce," he said with his hammer raised in the air, but before he could say another word he came down with all his might, not on the roofing nail, but on his thumb nail. He grabbed his thumb in pain, and it was squirting blood. He bled so much that Joel believes his blood stains are still on the decking of that roof to this day. But it taught him a great lesson.

"On second thought, I don't believe I'll tell you about Sister Pierce," he said, holding his throbbing thumb and grimacing in pain.

All of our experiences with Sister Pierce were not negative ones. Like the time she drove up to the parsonage with a big box full of frilly little dresses for Candy. She had found a sale and thought of my baby. The dresses were adorable and very much appreciated. I'm sure the Lord loved Sister Pierce, and he was honing us by her childish actions. It was a big part of our education and even though some of our dealings with her were difficult, the things she taught us about human nature are priceless.

One day we received a call from a neighboring pastor who lived out in the country just past the Arkansas line. He wanted to know if we were going to the fellowship meeting in Arkansas, and if we were, would we swing by and pick him up? We said "yes," and we did.

As we rode along, that dear pastor was delighted to have another pastor to discuss his problems with. He seemed to be at his wits end with some very difficult church members. Then he finally summed it up, and in his country way of talking he said; "Brother Joel, they're just *iggernut*, that 's all. . . .just plain *iggernut!*"

That precious man may not have been in command of the English language, but he got the point across, and I am inclined to agree with him. I believe he *hit the nail on the head*!

Chapter Eight

The Little Angel

The Little Angel

The church parking lot was deserted that Friday night as we drove up to let Tee and Betty out. The four of us had been to Dad Hemphill's church at Bawcomville for a special service, and they had left their car in the parking lot of our church in Bastrop. It was around 10:30 p.m. when we said our goodbyes. Joel and I waited for the Hodges to get into their car and pull out before we did, but they just stood there, silhouetted by the light of the moon, bending toward the faint glimmer of light coming from within their car. There was a note on the windshield and they kept reading it trying to absorb the contents that said;

"Come at once. Teressa is in the hospital but is doing fine. She drank some red furniture polish thinking it was soda pop."

Tee and Betty Hodges were new converts and had been coming to our church for only a few weeks. Anxious to become better acquainted, Joel and I invited them for a short trip to Bawcomville church and an evening of good Christian fellowship.

The Hodges had four small children, the youngest being baby Steven, just seven months old. There were three boys and eighteen-month-old Teressa, their only girl. On Wednesday night of this same week, while Tee was praying at the altar, giving his heart to the Lord, I held Teressa. She had big brown eyes, olive complexion and just a tuft of curly hair on top, resembling a cupid doll more than any child I have ever seen. She was absolutely adorable. The church had rejoiced that Wednesday evening. We were growing in number, and enthusiasm was at its peak.

Several of Betty's family who were already involved in our church, kept telling us that Tee and Betty were not Christians and urged us to try to win them. Joel and I visited them on several occasions and invited them to church. When they did come, it was with their whole hearts. They meant business, and everyone could tell it. It was an exciting time for our church family.

In order for the four of us to enjoy each others company on that Friday, we left our children with sitters. The Hodges' children had stayed with their grandparents, and now little Teressa was in the hospital! *"How can this be happening,?"* I asked the Lord in a state of shock.

After reading the note, the four of us rushed to the hospital deeply concerned, yet confident that all was well. Surely the outcome of this ordeal would be positive. The Lord wouldn't let anything happen to this precious family. Not now.

When we entered the hospital room where little Teressa was, we were not prepared for what we saw. She was under an oxygen tent in a state of semi-consciousness, struggling for her breath. The hospital had induced vomiting and the deadly stuff had filled her lungs and she was steadily becoming weaker.

Joel and I were speechless. After staying at the hospital until long after midnight and offering consolation and prayer, we left for home. More than anything Joel wanted to go to the church to pray and search for an answer to this tragic episode.

"Why Lord,?" he asked. *"If this child dies, what can I say to these young converts? How can I explain it, and what comfort can I possibly give to such an awesome loss?"*

It was such a puzzle, a heavy burden upon the shoulders of any pastor, especially one as young as Joel. We had stepped out on the promises of God and pointed this family toward a better way of life. And now this.

After staying up most of the night, Joel finally came to bed for a couple of hours' rest. Then early the next morning we rushed back to the hospital.

Little Teressa's color had changed from tan to a bluish grey. All the while, Tee and Betty were conveying a calm assurance, an unwavering child-like trust. And my faith, as I watched that tiny figure under the oxygen tent, was shattered.

"Was this precious child going to die?" I wondered.

I thought of my baby daughter, Candy. Like the Hodges she was our only little girl and the darling of our home. Grief overtook me as I tried to put myself in their place. *How could I stand to lose my baby?*

For two days and three nights that precious life hung in the balance. Then on Monday morning, the unthinkable happened. Teressa died.

Joel and I, Tee and Betty, several of their relatives, nurses and doctors as well, stood helplessly by and witnessed the last breath that passed those little lips.

In that moment of dark despair, like a tiny ray of light, Joel received an answer from the Lord. He took that remarkable couple by the hand, and with confidence that came straight from the throne, said to them: "Brother Tee, Sister Betty, we have read and studied about that place called heaven. Up until now it has been a faraway-place of little significance, but now it has just become very dear to you. You have an angel there, safe in the arms of Jesus, and waiting for you."

My Daddy Played The Guitar

What an awesome thought. My heart leaped with joy as I heard those words. Today, many years later, still finds the entire Hodges family dedicated Christians, and very active in their home churches. They are still finding out all they can about that place called heaven where their angel is. Not one time have they lost sight of their ultimate goal. Just knowing that Teressa is there has given their lives perfect aim in that heavenly direction.

It has given them determination to weather every storm that Christians face - even the storms of church upheavals and the disappointments of human failure that cause many to shipwreck. The Hodges are not deterred. They are on a journey to a glorious reunion with their little angel. The destination of their trip is not as far as when they started out, and oh, the joy of that meeting!

Prayer:
Father you are awesome! Your ways are perfect, even when we don't understand.

Thank you that you are mindful of your children and thank you for holding this precious family through their grief and bringing triumph out of tragedy!

Lord, I would love to be there when that long awaited reunion takes place. But if not, I will anticipate that happy time when I, too, will see that little angel once again.

Thank you Father for hope beyond the grave! In Jesus' name. Amen.

Chapter Nine

The Second Phase

The Second Phase

"Bubba your songs are never going to do all they *could* do until you and Breek are out there singing them yourselves."

Rusty's statement made my jaw drop.

The Happy Goodman Family had risen to the top in gospel music, and ever so often they would come by our house in Bastrop to hear Joel's latest songs. On this particular day they were on their way to Jonesboro, Louisiana to sing for our former governor, Jimmy Davis, at his yearly gospel music singing at the Jimmy Davis Tabernacle. Their big Silver Eagle bus finally came to a stop in our tiny driveway, after much maneuvering, and Goodmans and band members piled out. (Joel eventually had to cut down some trees in our yard and install a larger culvert to make our place more accessible to them).

Joel and I were standing under a shade tree in the yard, and with the help of Joel's guitar were singing Rusty our latest songs. When he realized how many songs Joel had written since he last saw us, that statement was forced from his lips.

The gift of song writing had come to Joel in a unexpected manner. He and I had been on a several-day fast, praying for gifts of the spirit and for a more dynamic preaching ministry. We were not satisfied with mediocrity in our church services. We knew that it would take a genuine move of God to draw people to Him. What came instead was songs. A flood gate was opened, and wonderful, singable, heartfelt songs began to pour through my husband.

My Daddy Played The Guitar

By now, my family, "The Goodmans" was recording two and three of our songs at a time on their albums, but Rusty saw that that wasn't enough. Joel and I were going to have to record these songs if all of them were to be heard.

I knew all too well what Rusty was saying on that fateful day. The truth is, when you make a record, then you have to travel and promote it in order to make it pay for itself. It becomes a cycle. You can't have one without the other. If you record, you travel and sing. If you travel and sing, you have to record so that your music will be played on the radio and folk will know who you are, or they won't bother to come to hear you in concerts. That's how it is - all or nothing!

The things that Rusty said only confirmed the stirrings that God had already placed in mine and Joel's hearts. In Joel's quite moments, the words of Jesus would surface in his spirit: "The field is the world." We knew the Lord was calling us from the important work of pastoring one of His little flocks, to other people and other places for a greater outreach.

The thought was exciting and at the same time brought feelings of uncertainty. To be quite honest, I did not want to hear it. Traveling and singing was what I had done all of my life before Joel came into the picture. I wasn't sure that I was ready to do that again. I loved my church, my home and my little town. But the die was cast.

Another phase of our ministry was already taking shape. It seemed that God had other plans for our lives, and I needed to trust Him. Besides, traveling and singing was part of who I was. I had been trained for it from my early childhood. So it wasn't something foreign, and when it did happen, I took to it like a fish to water.

Those were the events that led up to our leaving Bastrop, Louisiana. With new horizons looming before us, we gave up our church, thankful for ten wonderful years, and moved to Nashville, Tennessee, Music City U.S.A.

Chapter Ten

The Art Of Loving

The Art of Loving

I stood at the kitchen sink, gazing out the window at the hubbub of activity in our backyard. The birds were chirping and flitting, and the bushy tails were scampering from tree to tree. Bluejays were musically at war, staking their claims in the canopy of green. Summer had finally arrived and the sun was splashing its warm, golden rays with dappled beauty, dazzling everything it touched. For a moment I marveled at God's magnificent creation.

The flowers in bloom that I had so painstakingly planted were bursting forth in a kaleidoscope of color. Oddly enough my mood did not match the festive scene before me. The arrival of summer had not erased the feeling of dread that came with my last birthday in the dead of winter. Thirty-nine is not old. But that number announced loud and clear what was just ahead. I was about to step across the threshold of middle age and I didn't like it. The thought hit me hard and brought me face to face with my own mortality.

I certainly had no complaints. Life was good. Our move from Louisiana to Nashville had gone as smoothly as anyone could hope for. In the past seven years, we had accomplished a lot, working night and day. We were comfortably settled in our new home that Joel and our boys had built with their own hands. At my request Daddy had come up from Birmingham to help me with landscaping. He was so good at it. The two of us had made trip after trip to the nursery, hauling a variety of shrubs, planning, digging holes, sweating, and enjoying each other's company.

In the shade of the evening, Dad would get out his guitar and pick and sing. It was such a pleasant sound when he would take off on one of his favorite tunes; "Sadieee. . . .my little ladyeee." This brought back happy memories but it didn't change my pensive mood. My mind was on Mama Rogers. It was hard to believe that my dear grandmother was really gone. Today I had an overwhelming desire, an aching need to talk with her, and wondered how I had let her slip away without learning her secret. I needed to know how she became the lovable, gracious, most even-tempered person I had ever known. All of the virtues that made her who she was loomed before me at that moment as unattainable.

My Christian journey had become a struggle and seemed no different than that of the poor little salmon who spends a big part of his life going against the flow. You gain three feet and loose two or vice-versa, bruised, weary, and discouraged because you are constantly going against the current of popular opinion. Mine had been one continual self improvement plan that did not embrace the liberal lifestyles of modern society. I was still trying to guide my children, who were swiftly becoming adults, by example and gentle persuasion. What a challenge! And you only get one shot at it. I knew that before long my children would be grown and out on their own. Whatever I intended to instill in them by godly example had to be done now. There was no room for error. The sands of time were steadily moving, etching new paths and bringing about change. Change in me, change in my children and our home life. At this point I needed some answers. That's why I began to reflect on my grandmother.

Mama and Papa Rogers had lovingly taken me in with open arms when my parents divorced. They cushioned the separation from my mother with their affection. At the time that Dad and I moved in with them, they had several children still at home, to feed, clothe, and send to school. As I look back, I realize the extra work that our presence must have created; yet they included us and cared for me without hesitation.

Mama Rogers

The scenes that flash into mind when I think of my sweet grandmother are pleasant ones. The way she hummed around the house as she worked, bringing order to the chaos of howling grandbabies while helping one of her married daughters or daughters-in-law with their wash. I never saw a scowl or heard a harsh word from this gentle soul. That's not to say she couldn't demand orderly conduct from her children. She was an expert at that as well.

To rightfully describe Mama Rogers I would have to begin with her heart. It was as warm and ample as her lap that held and rocked me. I remember the well-scrubbed smell of soap, mixed with the delightful odors of starch and sunshine that were always with her and seemed to be her natural fragrance. The sound of her voice was as gentle and pleasant as laughter as she doled out a well-balanced diet of love and discipline to her children.

Most importantly, Mama Rogers was a Christian, and that was no secret. Everyone that knew her knew she had a personal relationship with the Lord, and it blessed our whole family. Mama Rogers was not overly vocal about her Christian experience. It was mostly her demeanor that won me over and played a big part in my wanting to become a Christian at an early age.

She was a true saint and not one to complain about the hardships of life. When I came along, our nation was still recovering from the Great Depression. Life was a challenge with little to look forward to, but as Mama Rogers worked around the house she hummed a tune as if everything was fine. And it was, because she made it so. I remember watching her carry bucket after bucket of water and wash mountains of clothes on her rub-board. The little three-roomed house we rented on Papa's meager wages from the Alabama coal mines had no running water or bathroom, and the only heat was from the wood cook stove in the kitchen. Even in the leanest of times I cannot remember missing a meal, though many were lean.

Mama taught her children to work too. Saturday was house cleaning day. The first time I was expected to do my share, it was met with lazy defiance; but it didn't matter that I was only seven, this was a job for everyone. Participation was not an option. So Mama Rogers handed me the dust rag and supervised my training.

I also remember the feelings of accomplishment when the work was done. When the house was sparkling clean, I was proud of my part in making it happen.

Washing the supper dishes was a nightly routine for the girls, which included me. Suppertime was when everything that had gone on during the day came to a close. You could always count on cornbread, (baked to a delicious crunchy brown) coleslaw, butterbeans, and iced tea with lemon. No matter what else was served, you could know for a fact this would be on Mama Rogers' table at supper time.

Supper for our family was a time of happy exchange while enjoying a meal of God's bounty. Discussions at the table included Daddy and Papa's experiences that day at the coal mine; and later stories of the people they'd met while on their insurance rounds. If nothing of interest had happened Papa would reach back and tell his favorite story about "Old Marble Head," the ghost that he had seen as a young man while traveling through the dark woods on horseback. Those were times that stand tall in my memories and helped me to know the importance of "breaking bread" with family.

After supper when the last tasty morsel was finished, Mama promptly left the room and the kitchen was turned over to my Aunt Joyce, six years older than I, June, my cousin, who was just a year or so younger than Joyce, and me. June was another of Mama and Papa's grandchildren that they were helping to raise.

We were expected to clear and clean the table. One would wash the dishes, one would dry, and the other would put them away. The job was never complete until the floor was swept and sometimes mopped. We girls were never as eager to get up from the table as we were to sit down to it. But the lesson was ingrained in us. Everyone had to do her part and if you ate you worked. I'm glad I learned that lesson; it has been very helpful to me. No matter where I am or what role I'm playing in life, that is one rule that always works!

I learned many things from my grandmother that had helped me through life, yet I had never probed her mind. Why hadn't I? I guess I took it for granted that she would always be there when I needed her. Even though I was raising my own family when she passed, I was too young to know the questions, much less look for answers. It's amazing how much the wisdom of our elders grows in our esteem as we get older.

It's like *Mark Twain* said about his father: "When I was sixteen my dad was so ignorant I could hardly stand to be around him. But by the time I was twenty-one, I was amazed at how much that old man had learned."

Mid-Life Crisis

Well at thirty-nine, I was out of answers. All I had was questions! I felt pulled in every direction. The demands of motherhood, wife, and homemaker were taking their toll on me. Not to mention our exhaustive concert schedule that was in full swing. If only I could bury myself in the safety of Mama Rogers' arms again. I needed her to assure me that everything would be all right. To hear her say that she had faced some of the same struggles, and that I would make it.

During this time I remember looking with detachment at the furnishings of my lovely new home. In the bathroom was the black and white wallpaper that had amused me, with chubby little cupids flying around. There were the black fixtures and gleaming tub that Joel and I had painstakingly chosen together, and all the beautiful things that I had dreamed of sharing with my own grandchildren one day.

"How many years do I have left?" I thought. *"Who will enjoy these things after I'm gone." "... how soon will that be?"*

I didn't know it then, but I was having an early mid-life crisis. However, the world keeps on turning and somehow I kept on going.

To make matters worse, while I was still in this heavy mood, a distant cousin of mine showed up at one of our concerts with a gift for me. It was a family portrait of Mama Rogers as a girl of sixteen, posing with all of her family plus her beau at the time - which was a very young Papa Rogers. My cousin had been tracing her family tree and came across the photo of my great grandmother and great grandfather, Grandma and Grandpa Hodge, the parents of Mama Rogers, with all of their children. The picture was a priceless treasure and I could hardly wait to be alone with it.

I studied the worn photo. There was the old home place in the background so typical of those turn-of-the-century family portraits, but my main point of interest was the young girl identified to me as

Mama Rogers. I focused all of my attention on her, her face, her hands, her size, yet nothing about her seemed familiar. Then I came to realize that the girl in the picture was Gertrude Hodges, *not yet* my grandmother. That girl was on the threshold of life with the fulfillment of her dreams just within grasp.

For days I studied that portrait as I ran my fingers lovingly over Mama and Papa Rogers. Seeing my dear grandmother as a young girl filled with hopes and dreams, and knowing her outcome was just too much for me. It added to my despair. It seemed that I was on a treadmill and it was going faster and faster. I was reminded of a scripture in the epistle of James that says; *"Whereas ye know not what shall be on the morrow. For what is your life? It is even a vapour, that appeareth for a little time, and then vanisheth away"* *(James 4:14).*

I am happy to report that I finally came out from under that dark cloud. It took a while but the Lord takes us *through* the valley. He never intended for us to camp there. It took a lot of searching and praying, but I came up with some answers of my own. It also became clear to me what Mama Rogers meant when she would often sigh and say, "It's a long road that never turns." And so it is. Life is like it is, not always like we want it to be.

I also understood that my grandmother had discovered and mastered one of the great secrets of all time, the art of loving. With skill and expertise she had stroked the chords of our souls with her love. Even though we knew of her relationship with the Lord, what we did not realize was that we had been indirect recipients of God's love as she weaved her beautiful, selfless life into ours. This understanding challenged me to love as she had loved. To be the true woman of God that she had been. But the big question remained. Could I ever achieve such a high mark? The goal was set before me by a real flesh-and-blood "Proverbs 31 woman." Sure Mama Rogers was human; she faced disappointment, opposition, and bone crushing adversity, as everyone does. Yet she remained unassuming and gallant. So it must be attainable, but can I do it?

Prayer:
Lord I'm trying!

Thank you Father that I knew such a lady and thank you that I was fortunate enough to have her as my grandmother, and to experience your love as it came through her to me. I am blessed! This woman's price is far above rubies. The heart of her husband trusted in her without disappointment. Strength and honor were her clothing and in her tongue was the law of kindness. Her children and grandchildren call her blessed, because she loved and feared the Lord. Amen.

Now, back to the question, "Can I achieve such a high mark set by my grandmother?" The answer is a resounding *yes*. It may take a lifetime but by God's grace and with His divine help I can attain it, and so can anyone else!

Chapter Eleven

Friends

Friends

My thoughts are never far from the things that I learned by example from my grandmothers. Their influence on me outweighs all others. One of the main things that stands out to me about Mama Rogers is that she rarely took time for herself and had few friends outside the family.

That's why Mrs. Jackson's visits were so special. She was my grandmother's best friend. It was through that friendship that I learned the importance of having someone who has the same interests to spend time with other than family.

Mrs. Jackson was an odd-looking little lady who was very short and was almost as round as she was tall. She had a funny, high-pitched voice and called Mama Rogers "Gertrude." I have no idea when or where their friendship developed, but one thing was evident: it was a real pleasure for them to be together. They laughed and talked like young girls. Mr. and Mrs. Jackson's visits were sporadic. They came by car, and we never knew when they would show up. But we kids knew that when Mrs. Jackson came we were not to get in the way, so we made ourselves scarce.

This special friendship lasted many years, and it showed a side of my grandmother that I hadn't seen before.

When Mrs. Jackson passed away, Joel and I were married and expecting Joey, our first born, so we could not go, but Mama Rogers' children came to Alabama to comfort her from as far away as Phoenix, Arizona. That's how special that friendship was, and it taught me how rewarding it can be to have someone who enjoys your company on your own merits.

There is no way to put a price on a good friendship, and it doesn't just happen. It requires time, patience and understanding. A true friend is a trust-worthy confidant. Someone you can talk to honestly and openly - a sounding board. To *have* a friend is to *be* a friend. Like the Scripture says; *"A man that hath friends must first show himself friendly" (Proverbs 18:24).*

My journey through life has been rewarded and enriched by my friends. I look back and recall different stages that I went through and realize how empty those times would have been without a friend to share the laughter, the secrets, even the disappointments.

In grammar school in Evansville, I had a special friend named Betty. Then at church I had other special friends; Norma McCoy from that same area, and Peggy Rogers (Butler) from the church that I attended when I lived in Asheville, North Carolina. I shared many happy times in school and church activities with those girls.

Then in Fultondale, Alabama, in Junior-high, there was the unforgettable Snooky Gallagher, a whirlwind of freckled energy. We were basketball cheerleaders, next door neighbors, and were in the same homeroom in school.

Snooky and I shared some of the most exciting times of my growing up. At the ages of fifteen and sixteen you experience the new-found feelings of adulthood without the burden of responsibility. Those were carefree and joyous times when life was just one big party, with hayrides, wiener roasts, ballgames, beauty contests, and falling in and out of love every other week.

Later when Joel and I were married, we formed friendships with couples from our church that have spanned decades and hundreds of miles, endured many a change, and are still intact today. Those dear friends have been in our lives for so long, they are now like family to us. The names of several of them have and will crop up in this book as I recount experiences that we've had together through the years. We've laughed, cried and prayed with each other, been on vacations together, and have had some interesting things happen to us along the way. Some have been funny, even downright hilarious. At times I'm afraid we tend to take ourselves too seriously. I know I have. But there are times that we need to loosen up, join in the fun, and laugh even at ourselves! Like the Scripture says; *"A merry heart doeth good like a medicine" (Proverbs 17:22).*

There are also things that happen with friends that aren't so funny - things that have to be reconciled - like the time I had to apologize to a very dear friend of mine.

Chapter Twelve

Feathers In The Wind

Feathers In The Wind

*T*here is a despicable little character from Grimm's fairytales that had a saying, "Sticks ands stones may break my bones but *words* will never hurt me." His name, Rumpelstiltskin.

When I first heard that saying I was just a child. It was a new idea, a thought that I had never entertained before, and I pondered over it. It sounded true, but something just wasn't right about that saying. In years to come, not too far down the road of life, I realized what had me stumped about this concept. It was a half-truth. Sticks and stones *can* break bones, but *words* can break too. Words can break hearts. They can break spirits. Words can, and do, break friendships, marriages, and homes. Another thing I came to realize is that broken bones heal much quicker than these other things do.

The Dream

It was early morning, still dark outside, and I found myself wide awake with a pounding heart. I had had a disturbing dream, and it brought me out of a sound sleep. This was no ordinary dream; it was a nudge from the Lord. I woke up knowing that I had to make a long distance phone call, and try to make amends for an old wound that I had inflicted, some fifteen years back, on a friend that we had pastored in Bastrop. Though I hadn't seen this person in over ten years, there needed to be an apology for some harsh words that I had spoken. It was a conversation that I had completely forgotten, but she hadn't. And neither had the Lord. Not all dreams are from the Lord, but this one was. It placed me in that old setting with all of my senses highly sharpened, and old feelings aroused.

Betty was a faithful member of our church and a true Christian. She never missed service if she could help it, and she loved Joel and me. She was always there for us from the start, and she and I became very close and had great times together. Joel and I enjoyed being with Betty and Jerry, whether at church, in their home, or fishing in Bussy Break.

When mine and Joel's ministry started shifting more toward music, she was devastated. She knew that we would be leaving sooner or later, and it broke her heart. Because of this, she'd made some negative remarks on the subject.

By nature I am an impulsive person. I have been known to say and do things on the spur of the moment which can sometimes be a problem. I have had to learn to press against my nature, and am still learning. Like the child that gets burned when he reaches out to the fire, I don't enjoy the consequence.

In my younger days my impulsive nature was much more prominent. I had that "get back" attitude. I used that infantile practice with my friend Betty, not realizing the pain that I had caused her.

Days and weeks before the dream, I had been spending more time in prayer and Bible study.

In reading the epistle of James, I came across the Scriptures that say, *". . . . let every man be swift to hear, slow to speak, slow to wrath. . . ." (James 1:19)*. *"If any man among you seem to be religious, and bridleth not his tongue . . . .this man's religion is vain" (James 1:26)*. Then he said, ***"if any man offend not in word, the same is a perfect man, and able also to bridle the whole body" (James 3:2)***.

The Lord showed me in prayer how my attitude needed adjusting, and it was causing me pain in different areas that I wasn't even aware of. (When the Lord has shown me things about my imperfections I have tried to correct them. I don't like to suffer).

James, the apostle, challenged me to strive for perfection. He even showed me the way - not that any of us has arrived, but he pointed me in that direction. Surely it must be attainable for Jesus himself told us; *"Be ye, therefore, perfect, even as your **Father, who is in heaven, is perfect"** (Matthew 5:48)*. Well I certainly have a long way to go to reach that point. But it doesn't hurt to try.

Back to the dream. I dreamed that I was in the sanctuary approaching Betty. Something she had said to me previously had me agitated. My thoughts were upon getting even. I had a straight pin in my hand, and when I greeted her, I planned to *accidently* scratch her with it. I could see in my mind that it would cause just a small, white scrape, nothing more. Mind you, this was just a dream, and something I had never actually done or thought about doing. But I believe the Lord was showing me that my plan to "jab" my Christian sister with *words* was devious and detrimental. It was as if I were using *words* as an implement no different than a straight pin!

The next part of my dream made me gasp. She was holding her index finger out to me, and it was cut to the bone. The wound was red, infected, and gaping. Horrified at what I had done, I was immediately overcome with compassion. Then I awoke with a pounding heart, filled with remorse.

It was hours after I woke up from that dream before I could make the call, so I waited, and watched the clock. One thing for sure, I could not go another day without trying to fix this.

At 8:00 a.m. that same morning I dialed her number. "Sister Betty, this is a voice from your past" I said. "Oh, Sister Hemphill, I was just vacuuming the floor and thinking about you," she responded warmly. When she said that, it made my job much easier because I could see that God was working on both ends of the line. "Well, I've called to apologize for some things that I said that hurt you. I want to pour oil in that wound and bind it up with love." She was so sweet and gracious and very glad to hear from me. We talked freely and openly about the past. She let me know that she couldn't understand what was happening when we gave up the church to sing and evangelize. I told her that even I didn't fully understand at the time. But as the saying goes, hindsight has 20/20 vision!

It is easy now to see the hand of God moving to expand our horizons - leading, teaching, and maturing us for a more effective and broader ministry. I assured Sister Betty that our time spent in Bastrop with them was some of the most rewarding and important time of our ministry. The years spent there were foundational. That conversation was long past due. Our friendship was renewed and the incident put to rest. We have since moved on with our lives. We remain friends to this day and enjoy phone conversations from time to time.

Re-Examining My Words

God is awesome. He really cares. He cared for the precious friend that I had wounded, and He cared for me, a struggling Christian. He cared enough to show me my mistake, even though it was several years old, and He gave me the chance to rectify it.

As careful as I can be, I still have to apologize now and then for a careless remark, sometimes a mere jest, that I later regret making. Words said in anger, or haste, are like feathers in the wind. There is just no way to take them back. They also taste much different, the second time around, when you have to eat them. It's good to know that I'm not responsible for the words of others, what they might say to me; it is just my response, my own words that for which I am accountable. It's hard to overstate the importance of words, for Jesus said, *"By thy **words** thou shalt be justified, and by thy **words** thou shalt be condemned" (Matt. 12:37).*

I'll never forget trying to obey the Scripture that says *". . . study to be quiet" (I Thess. 4:11).* It was a real challenge when I started trying to put that one into practice. Up until that point, I felt it my duty, and obligation, to state my opinion on every subject - with gusto! I really had to *study* to be quiet, and there were times I thought I would explode if I didn't voice my opinion in every conversation around me. Funny thing, it didn't take long to find out that no one seemed to mind that I was silent, or even noticed. Conversations continued to flow, and seldom was I asked my opinion. What an eye opener! Now, when my opinion is desired, I treat the opportunity with great respect and try to interject words of wisdom - *in short form.*

Having said this, try as I may, every once in a while, when my guard is down, I will say the wrong thing at the wrong time, and wind up having to say "I'm sorry." Those experiences are so distasteful that it causes me to think twice before I speak, *most* of the time.

Before closing this chapter there is one more thing that I need to share. It is about using the Lord's name as slang. It might seem harmless, even to the average Christian, to say in passing; Oh Lord! or, Oh God!, or, how about, Oh Jesus!

115

My Daddy Played The Guitar

I found myself doing this at times, but when I really wanted the Lord's attention I wondered if I wasn't like the little boy who cried wolf. When I pray, I want the Lord to listen, not tune me out. It took some doing but I broke myself of that habit as well and feel good about it. A good rule that I follow now is that I only speak the Lord's name when I am speaking *to* Him or *about* Him. It is very important for me to please the Lord, and not offend Him in word or deed. Hosea said, *"Take with you words, and turn to the Lord; say to him, take away all iniquity, and receive us graciously:..." (Hosea 14:2).*

Prayer:

> *"Let the words of my mouth and the meditation of my heart be acceptable in your sight, O Lord my strength, and my Redeemer" (Ps. 19:14).*

> *"Lord, give me wisdom and help me to be "swift to hear, slow to speak, and slow to wrath" (James 1:19).*

Heavenly Father, don't let me be deceived into thinking that all is well, and that I am growing in Christ, if I haven't taken care of that unruly little member called the tongue. Help me to speak words that encourage, strengthen, and bless. Thank you Father for your help in these matters, in Jesus name I pray. Amen.

Chapter Thirteen

Pick A Number

"Pick a Number"

*T*he white Lincoln Continental rolled to a stop at the top of our driveway. It had "Lou" written in cursive on the front license plate and rightly so. Lou Hildreth, my friend, and also our booking agent, had come for me and we were about to take an excursion. She had called the week before with a proposal.

"LaBreeska, a gospel disc jockey is having a big day in Shelbyville next week and wants you and me to come and be a part of it. He plans to broadcast his program live from a building in the downtown area. He has asked several gospel music personalities to participate such as Wendy Bagwell, Don Butler and others along with you and me. We will be interviewed on the radio and he wants to give away some albums. What he wants you to do is bring a few boxes of your new book and have an autograph party. Do you think you could go?" I hurriedly checked our schedule and found that we would be home, so I gladly took her up on it.

Lou Wills Hildreth is a classy lady. She comes from a well-known family of singers and musicians of both gospel and country music. Her cousin, Bob Wills, was responsible for originating a sound that dominated country western music back in the 40's called "western swing." That innovative sound brought Bob Wills and his band, The Texas Playboys, to the forefront in popularity. It even took them to Hollywood and landed them parts in cowboy movies. Lou's father, Bob's first cousin, led his family in the direction of gospel music and they were quite successful as well.

Lou has dedicated her life to helping promote gospel music. She is well connected and highly respected. If truth be known, she planted the idea in Ed the D.J.'s mind about my autograph party. That is just her way - always figuring an angle to help anyone and everyone in gospel music. (She was recently inducted into the Gospel Music Hall of Fame).

For the special event in Shelbyville, I had chosen a white linen suit to wear, with a leopard design, silk scarf tied around my neck. Lou was smartly dressed in a wine colored suit. We were "decked to the nines" and would be riding in style in Lou's new car.

When I started to get into the car it surprised me when Lou *insisted* that I drive. I looked at her questioningly, then shrugged and said "Sure, why not?"

I got under the wheel and had no more than cleared our driveway, about to get on the intestate, when I asked, "Which way do we go, Lou?" When I turned to look at her she had this blank look on her face and answered, "Don't you know?" Then, "bingo" the lights came on and suddenly I understood why she was so eager to put *me* under the wheel. She didn't want me to know that she knew *nothing* about directions.

If I drove and got us there, then perhaps she would never have to divulge her embarrassing secret. What Lou *didn't* know however, was that if *she* was bad with directions, she had just found someone worse. I used to get lost in the little town of Bastrop!

Of course those were the days before the computer society. There were no cell phones or G.P.S. gadgets, and very few car phones. No, it wasn't the horse-and-buggy days. We were enjoying modern transportation, but communication was lacking in comparison with today.

When the truth finally soaked in on us, we did the only thing left to do. We found the nearest service station, just a stone's throw from my house, and asked for directions to Shelbyville, only 45 miles from home!

Before long our spirits were soaring. We were headed in the right direction, gently gliding along under powder blue skies. There wasn't a cloud in sight. It was a perfect day, and we were going to have a great time. Nothing could spoil that now.

When we arrived in Shelbyville we drove straight to the building without a hitch and discovered quite a bit of activity already stirring. Ed, the disc jockey, was playing gospel music on the air and inviting people from all around to "drop in" for refreshments, free records, and autographs.

As a steady stream of people milled around, I set up a table of my books and thought, "This is really nice!" I was busy shaking hands and signing autographs and hadn't noticed when Ed called Lou to the microphone. The next thing I knew, he was asking Lou all about her family, the famous Wills' Family and her cousin Bob Wills from Texas. Lou was telling about her involvement in Gospel music and how she had gotten her start. Then Ed said, "Now, Lou, it is time to give away a record. I want you to pick a number and whoever has that lucky number wins this album." Well, Lou was just splendid and in complete control. She sweetly replied, "Ed, I already have a number; it is number seven, God's lucky number." The record was given away and , to say the least, I was impressed with Lou. I thought, "I want to have a number ready when he calls me up, too," so in my mind I selected number three.

A short time later Ed called me to the microphone. He began flattering me with nice words about my accomplishments. "LaBreeska, how did you ever find time in your busy schedule of traveling and singing to write this book?"

He had read it and was telling everyone how good it was, and had built me up as an intelligent, self-assured woman. He complimented the discipline I must have possessed while doing all this writing. I was really feeling intellectual.

Then it came time to give away another album, and I smiled confidently because I already had my number, just like Lou. My mistake was that I wasn't listening when Ed said, "Pick a number between fifteen and twenty."

When I came up with the number three, Ed turned visibly pale. He began to stutter and stammer around and said, "No, no LaBreeska." By then I knew I had said something wrong but I didn't know what, and it blew my mind. Ed said quickly, "Pick another number. Pick another number."

Now totally confused, I blurted out, "Thirteen." Ed was by now devastated. He was just plain speechless, and I was *mortified*. I glanced around at Lou and she had lost all composure. She was bent-over, laughing and wiping tears. Wendy Bagwell was coughing and laughing and slapping his leg.

It seemed like an eternity before Ed finally found his voice. He looked at me and started showing me on his fingers slowly and deliberately. "LaBreeska, you can pick fifteen, sixteen, seventeen . . . ." I quickly said one of those numbers, and in a daze found the way back to my chair. To say the least, the rest of the day was uneventful after that.

Two weeks later Joel and I, along with our group, were traveling in our bus on the way to Tuscaloosa, Alabama to sing at the annual Fireman's Gospel Concert. I knew we were going to be with Wendy Bagwell that night and also knew that if I didn't tell Joel what had happened in Shelbyville, Wendy would. When I approached Joel, he was lying on his bunk, in our back room, as the bus continued to make its way toward Tuscaloosa. He was reading the paper and I went in and lay down beside him.

"Honey, there's something I want to tell you about what happened in Shelbyville the other day . . . ." By the time I finished the story, both of us were in the floor laughing and wiping tears. That was the first time I had seen anything funny about it at all. Up until then, it was not a subject that I was ready to discuss or even think about.

It was a good thing that I told Joel and our group about it first, because Wendy Bagwell, being the yarn spinner that he was, had a ball at my expense. He relayed the whole episode to the nine-thousand-plus congregation at our singing that night.

Through the years I have had several embarrassing moments, but I will have to say the one in Shelbyville wins the prize!

Prayer:
Lord you sure have a way of bringing us back to earth! Thank you for reminding me that I am just human, with short comings as well as accomplishments. Thank you also for teaching me not to take myself too seriously. Amen!

LaBreeska

Erskine Rogers
My Dad

Gussie Mae Goodman Rogers
My Mother

My paternal grandparents Mama and Papa Rogers.

"A picture is worth a thousand words."

Mama and Papa Goodman

Aunt Fay, Mama Rogers and Mother having fun on the porch of our house in the coal mining camp.

Goodman Family Trio
Stella, Howard and Eloise

Mother

Aunt Joyce and Me

Me at age 13

Daddy holding
his son Buddy to the left and his
grandson Joey, our first born.

Daddy, Lila, Baby Jane, and
Me at age 7

Dad and his two brothers:
Herman (Red) to the left and younger brother Jim to the right.

We were told to
look solemn in
this picture!

Joel & Me in the
rockers

Joey, Candy &
Trent behind

Me, Mother,
Mama Goodman,
Aunt Stella

Joey with his
Grandpa and
Nanny Lila

Family Publicity Shots

Joel and Me with our children, Joey, Trent and Candy

Joel and LaBreeska

Me and Candy

Our three children before
they left the "nest"

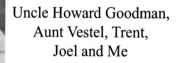

Uncle Howard Goodman,
Aunt Vestel, Trent,
Joel and Me

Travels

On top of Mount Sinai Egypt
Watching the sunrise

Aloha from Hawaii

Trying to do
the hula!

I still can't
believe I got
this close to
the molten
lava from the
volcano!

Charlene & Me

Joel with a couple
of the singers from
Kodak Hula Show

Our first trip to
Hawaii with all
the group

All the lovely flower
arrangements in the
restaurants & hotel
lobbies were fresh cut.

Israel

Being presented with the Jerusalem Award by the Minister of Tourism. Left to right, Tim McKeithen, Jasmine, Candy, Me, Joel, Mr. Etzion and Polly Grimes.

Pastor Gerald Mangun blessing Joel and Me on the Mt. of Olives. Our friend Jerry Johnson on the right.

Joel blowing
the shofar
at the Western
Wall in
Jerusalem

Brother
Mangun
at far right

With our dear friends
Guy and Jean Garner
from Ashdod, Israel

Me and Clyde the
Camel with one of the
many Solomans
in Egypt

We found my purse two blocks away in busy London, England. Wes Newton, Me, Wallace Nelmes and David Hall

In the home of friends in Belfast, N. Ireland

Joel and me with mayor of Bally-money, N. Ireland

Grandchildren

Joel and Me with Jasmine, our first

Joel's Mom, Grandma Hemphill, with Great-Granddaughter Madeleine Grace, Joel and Me

Jasmine, Me, Madeleine and Nick putting candles on William's (in front) birthday cake

Nick caught a fish
at family reunion

Madeleine
Grace

William

Sarah

Some of My Favorite Pictures

Me rocking
Grandbaby Taylor

My dad
with three
of his great-
grandchildren
Jasmine,
Madeleine &
Taylor

Trent and
Madeleine

Joel and me
recording

Joel's sister Gayle waiting
back stage with us

Joel with our dear friends
Howard and Lou Wills Hildreth

Our three children Trent, Candy, and Joey with Joel and Me.

Joel and Me with an old car we restored

Trent and wife Bethni, Joey and wife Sue Ann with President Geroge W. Bush

Christmas at Candys

All our Grandchildren
Sarah, Jasmine, Taylor, Madeleine, Nick and William

Children and Grandchildren
Nick, Bethni, Me, Joey, Joel, Candy, Sarah
Jasmine, Taylor, William, Madeline, Trent

Chapter Fourteen

Ole Flo

Ole Flo

*I*t was Saturday morning, bright and sunny and full of promise. Bastrop was having a big "arts and crafts day." I was on my way and could hardly wait to get there.

The previous day Joel and I had come from our home in Nashville to visit his family in West Monroe. Whenever we had a free weekend from our concert tours we rarely missed an opportunity to drive down to see his parents. It was so rewarding to go back to Joel's "roots." The pace in his hometown was much slower than what we had become accustomed to. Just to see familiar places and faces, the church that his dad had founded, and childhood friends, had a healing affect on both of us.

We had left all of that a few years back and traded it for the "fast lane." Our gospel music travels had become extensive and grueling, and being cramped up in our tour bus several days a week, along with eight other people, was confining and made each of us want to escape to the wide open spaces the first chance we got. Our teenaged children had already claimed Nashville as home. Most of the time they stayed behind enjoying church activities and school friends, while Joel and I headed for Louisiana for a few days respite. Then there was Bastrop, only 30 miles from Monroe. Even though we had moved away, Joel and I had never severed ties with the town, nor our friendships that were made during that time.

Charlene, one of my close Bastrop friends, had excitedly informed me of the big day of festivities and urged me to come when I called to let her know that I was in Monroe. Now on this gorgeous

June morning, I was clipping merrily along in my automobile looking forward to an exciting time. Since most of Bastrop would turn out for this special occasion, I was sure to meet up with many friends from the past. Filled with eager anticipation, I had a song in my heart and a smile on my face, and the closer I got to Bastrop the lighter I felt. When I arrived at Charlene's house, she was as eager as I to get going. Leaving my car parked in her driveway, I got in with her and away we went.

Sure enough, by the time we reached town it was already buzzing. Folk were streaming in from all directions, so much so that we had to park a good way down a side street. Then we eagerly joined the bustle of activity on the sidewalk with the others. The town square and much of main street was blocked off for the vendors and the throngs who were expected to show up. There were so many people already there that the going was slow, and running into *my* old friends even slower. But it was great just being there. I had spent a big part of my life in that little town. Bastrop was *my* town. I loved it. At one point I didn't believe that it could ever be replaced, and it would certainly never be erased from my heart.

My childhood had been unstable and without roots. My school years were spent in eleven different schools in eight states. There was hardly a place in my past that I could revisit and see old friends; therefore, when we moved to Bastrop to raise our children and become the shepherd over one of God's little flocks, that stability and sense of belonging was hard for me to give up.

But I found out early in life that nothing stays the same. If we don't move when the Lord says move, we become stagnant and out of the center of His will. To be all that He intends us to be, we must be *willing* and *pliable,* even when we don't understand.

Ole Flo

Uprooting and leaving my home, my town, my church and friends was hard, but I was willing. Time and space have a way of taking care of the upheavals that we go through. That is exactly what had happened to me. Before long I came to accept my new roll in life, and Nashville as home. Things were going well for us, and our three children, Joey, Trent and Candy, had adapted to their new surroundings with ease.

Now here I was, once again, back in Bastrop enjoying one of my long-time friends and having a ball. We were going to make a day of it . . . .or so I thought.

The Wedding

We couldn't have been there an hour when Charlene dropped a bombshell on my spirits. "Breeska my brother is getting married in Lake Village, Arkansas today at 2:00 and I promised him and my family that I would be there. It's just a couple of hours from here. If you'll go with me we can hurry and be back in plenty of time to enjoy the rest of the day."

She went on, "If we left now we could visit them before the wedding, then head back as soon as the ceremony is over."

My heart sank. I didn't want to leave, but I also didn't want to stay in town by myself, that wouldn't be any fun. Reluctantly, I agreed to go with her even though at a wedding in Lake Village, Arkansas was the last place I wanted to be. Since we had to go, there was no time like the present.

The quicker we left, the quicker we could return, and the day wouldn't be a total wash out. When we drove away I watched from my side mirror as Bastrop and all of its festivities slowly faded out of sight.

Disappointment soon dissolved, and in no time we were laughing and talking as ususal. Charlene and I could always find plenty to talk about, and we had a lot of catching up to do since we had last been together.

Her's and Jerry's three children, Theresa, Rita and Danny, were close to the same ages as our three. We could always compare notes on them. And Charlene was sincerely interested in where we had been in concert and what Joel's latest song was.

Then of course I had to hear all about different ones of the church and how they were doing. Usually my first question was: "How is Sister Vertie Mae?"

Her name was Vertie Mae but the church lovingly called her *Sister* Vertie Mae. When she smiled, her whole face lit up and you could hardly see her eyes. She loved everyone. Her love for the church and the things of God drew the church family to her like a magnet. Sister Vertie Mae was a saint of God and she, along with several others, were true church mothers in every sense of the word. The ten years that we pastored her was a delight. She was one of very few people that called me "Beeky" like my Papa Rogers. That endeared her to me even more.

R.D. and Vertie Mae lived several miles out in the country, close to the Arkansas state line. She could take any mundane day and make it an exciting event with one phone call. The parsonage phone, hanging on the wall in a tiny area we called the hall, would ring.

On the other end of the line she would say; "Beeky, how about you and Brother Joel and the kids coming out for lunch?" Now "lunch" would be a feast of garden vegetables of all descriptions, with fried chicken or pork chops, topped off with her special coconut cake and pecan pie. It would also last all day.

Sister Vertie Mae had a hunger for the Word of God and loved to ask Joel about certain scriptures pertaining to the end of time. Usually before the day came to a close, we would sing a few songs and have prayer.

Going to R.D.'s and Vertie Mae's house was always a treat. When we had visiting ministers, she loved to cook and have us bring them out.

They had a modest house built on the land that had been in R.D.'s family for many years. It was the old Fillingame homeplace. The yard was dotted with gigantic pecan trees, and they were loaded with pecans at certain times of the year.

Roscoe

When Sister Vertie Mae invited us to bring my Uncle Howard Goodman and Aunt Vestal out, he loved their place. He enjoyed picking up pecans, cracking and eating them. What I remember vividly about going there was their old Catahoula Curr dog that just sat around in the yard watching us. He looked ominous with his one blue eye (almost white) and one brown eye. This breed of dog is also known as the Glass-Eyed Curr.

Most of the time, when we were outside, I tried to keep him in sight. He reminded me of someone's saying about a certain dog they knew. They said that he was so ornery, he would befriend you for years just to get to bite you one time. That's how I felt about Roscoe. Come to find out, I wasn't wrong. Sister Vertie Mae came to church one night telling us about hearing a noise on her roof. She went outside, to find her insurance man on top of the house. Roscoe had him treed. When the race was on, the salesman, just barely out of the dog's reach, had jumped upon the banister, shinnied up the lattice-work of the wrought-iron post, and landed on the roof of the porch.

After that, I knew I'd never trust a dog with one brown eye and one blue eye.

R.D. and Sister Vertie Mae sang specials with her two sisters and brother. They called themselves the Layton Family, and patterned their style after the Chuck Wagon Gang, singing many of their songs. In fact the Layton's, which was Vertie Mae's maiden name, made up a big part of our church, either directly or indirectly.

Aunt Lura Mae was another wonderful church mother who was an inspiration and an example to me. She was Sister Vertie Mae's aunt, as well as aunt to a host of other church members, and Charlene's mother-in-law. Sister Lura Mae was a woman of God and I loved her. Usually when I saw Charlene, I wanted to know how she and Uncle Rush were doing. She was a delight to pastor and her carrot cake was phenomenal. When Joel first bit into Sister Lura Mae's carrot cake he said, "Now I know why God made carrots!"

Charlene kept me up to date on our dear friends. In my inquiry, I would ask about Roy and Jeanette. Roy and Joel's birthday's were within days of each other; they were the same age and still remained hunting buddies.

When we first met, Roy and Jeanette had been married only a few months, and Jeanette was, and still is, a beauty. She had honey blond hair that hung loosely around her shoulders. She was fair, with perfectly straight teeth, and sang specials at church. Our friendship with this couple remained strong all through the years, but our dear Roy has since been laid to rest.

On the way to the wedding that day, we laughed and reminisced. Then before we knew it, Charlene and I were in Lake Village searching for the house where it was to take place in. We eventually found it, but to our dismay, we found that no one seemed to be in a hurry to get on with the program but us. The ceremony was far from being on schedule. By the time they said "I do" it was looking more like 3:00 instead of 2:00, and I was beginning to see the "hand writing on the wall."

The Caught Feeling

Eventually, Charlene and I said our goodbyes, made our exit, and pointed the nose of her new Lincoln toward Bastrop. On the way back I was getting antsy. The road luckily was clear of traffic except for an occasional farmer or trucker that we quickly passed and left behind.

But the day was getting by. Finally I said, "Step on it Charlene." And she did. Just as she did, a patrol car came from out of nowhere with flashing blue lights, and started gaining on us.

It was something that neither of us had expected and it took our breath away. We had that "caught feeling" that hits you right in the pit of the stomach. Charlene panicked! "What am I going to do?" she asked breathlessly. I was trying to stay calm. "Joel sometimes talks them out of it," I responded hurriedly. "What does he say?," she asked. I was searching my brain. "Well, I heard him tell one officer that he didn't realize he was going that fast; he was just going along with the flow of the traffic."

By now we were stopped, and Charlene was being motioned to get out of the car. She wound up at the back of our vehicle with the officer, and I was afraid to turn around and look back. All I could do was patiently wait for her to get back into the car. In a few minutes, she opened the door and slid under the wheel as the officer pulled out, passed us, and left.

Rarely have I seen Charlene speechless, but she was visibly shaken, and silent. I was the first to speak.

"What happened?" "Did you get a ticket?"

When she finally found her voice, she exhaled real big and answered, "No, I just got a warning." I was relieved and said, "Well that's great! Did you talk the officer out of it?" Then Charlene turned and looked at me and said "Breeska, that state trooper was the tallest woman I ever saw!" She went on. "I did like you said. I told her that I didn't realize how fast I was going, that I was just going along with the flow of the traffic."

"It must have worked" I said. "You didn't get a ticket!"

"Well I didn't know if she was going to write me up or not," she said. "When I told her that, she looked down at me and said: 'That sounds good, but there is no one on this road but you and me!' Breeska, I could've died! She was tough. She said, 'I'm not going to give you a ticket this time, but you had *better* slow it down!' That's when she let me go."

The two of us sat there for a minute trying to digest what had just happened. Then Charlene started the engine and we took off . . . .slowly. It didn't take long, however, for her to get over the shock of being stopped and the embarrassment of her conversation with the lady trooper. Then we had a good laugh. We were happy that we didn't get a ticket, and all is well that ends well.

That actually isn't the end of this story. When we got back to Bastrop the crowd had gone home. About the only thing left was a vendor or two dismantling and packing up their wares. Paper was scattered in the streets, blowing around in the breeze. We were tired anyway. It had been a full day, and very eventful.

I soon left Charlene in her driveway and took off for Monroe. When she went inside and told Jerry and her kids the story about being stopped by the woman trooper, they howled! They thought that was one of the funniest stories they had ever heard. From then on, when Charlene's family wanted to tease her, all they had to do was call her *"Ole Flo."*

Chapter Fifteen

Facing The Unexpected

Facing The Unexpected

When we entered the Mayo home that day Joel and I were at a loss for words. What do you say to a couple who has just lost a child?

When we heard that the single-engine plane that Ken was piloting malfunctioned, causing it to crash and taking his life, we hurried to be with his parents as soon as we could.

Brother David and Sister Molly Mayo are veterans when it comes to serving the Lord and their fellowman. For decades they have pastored churches in North Louisiana. They have seen a lot of tragedies and helped others deal with grief, but losing one of their own children was a blow. It pained us to see them hit so hard with one of life's unexpected tragedies.

After moving to Nashville, for years Joel and I wintered in Monroe at our farm on the Bayou, and Joel taught the Bible class at Brother Mayo's church. They were our pastors for two or three months out of the year and are very dear to us.

The plane crash, was a blow to everyone who knew them. Ken Mayo was a promising young minister with a beautiful wife and three small children. A man full of life, hopes, plans, and dreams; then in a moment's time, he was taken from our midst. It didn't seem possible.

All any of us could do was just stand beside this dear couple and hope they could draw strength and comfort from our presence. And I'm sure they did. But their main source of strength was the word of God that they had lived by and taught for so long.

Some two months before Ken's accident, Molly Mayo found a scripture in the Bible that really spoke to her. It was Luke 7:33 where Jesus said:

> *"Blessed is he who is not offended because of me."*

The scripture hung in her mind and she wondered why the Lord was bringing it to her attention. She even made mention of it to her husband and children. Then she made a copy of that Bible verse and stuck it on the front of her refrigerator so she could see it daily. Sister Molly had no way of knowing that God was preparing her with something to hold onto when her unexpected storm would try to blow her way.

Molly Mayo doesn't play favorites with her children. She will let you know in a split second that she loves all of them the same. Evidently she and Brother David did something right. They raised two ministers of the gospel, Michael and Ken. Another son, David Jr., is a fine Christian man, and a worship leader at his dad's church. Anise their only daughter is the church organist. But the whole family knew and accepted the fact that Ken *was* special to his parents because he doted on them. He called his mother almost daily. Ken, being a pastor himself, had much in common with his mom and dad. They enjoyed each other's company and often made trips together. Losing Ken would leave a void in this aging couple's life that could never be replaced.

There were others at the Mayo home when Joel and I arrived that day: Anise and "Poochie," her husband, very dear friends of ours for many years, along with several other relatives and church friends. We were all there to support and encourage, but I don't believe any of us were prepared for what happened next.

140

Sister Molly, sick with grief, and still reeling from the untimely death of that precious son, looked around the room and made this statement; "I am ***not offended*** at the Lord." This was her stand. Instead of encouraging her, she blessed us that day with that bold declaration.

She was letting us know that she *trusted* her God, even though she did not understand His purpose or His plan. In her vulnerable state of pain she landed on the words of Jesus her Savior. And I will add one of my favorite verses from King David:

> *"Great peace have they who love thy law, and*
> *nothing shall **offend** them" (Ps. 119:165).*

Sister Molly applied his words to her own situation. She would not be offended at God the Father and would bear her cross just as Jesus our example did when he prayed in the garden:

> *"Father, not my will but thine be done."*

This dear saint's world was shaken but not her faith in God. It was well grounded.

> *"The Lord gave, and the Lord hath taken away;*
> *blessed be the name of the Lord" (Job 1:21).*

The Mayo's suffered the loss of their darling son but not without hope. From the word of God they knew that one day they would embrace him again. This comforting knowledge saw them through their trial by fire. Their faith and courage is a monument that stands tall to the rest of their children and to those of us who witnessed it.

In view of the Mayo tragedy, I was reminded of another plane crash that took another favored son when I was barely a teen. Sad to say, the outcome was totally opposite from the one I have just described. I'm referring to the funeral of my cousin B.J.

Another Plane-Crash

B.J. was making a career in the Air Force. He was the eldest son, handsome, intelligent, and beloved of his father.

On the day that he was flying for his "wings," an insignia worn by pilots, his plane went down and B.J. was killed in the crash. The big day of celebration turned to one of deep, dark mourning, leading up to a day I'll *never* forget.

It wasn't until after the memorial service when we all gathered at the home of B.J.'s parents, that I understood what was taking place, and it chilled me to the bone.

My uncle, B.J.'s father was an alcoholic, a fact that had eluded me up until then. His addiction had overshadowed his family and had taken the joy out of their home, even though he had provided well for them. On the day of the funeral he was completely saturated. What we saw and heard from him filled us all with fear and dread. My uncle, cut to the heart, wounded, offended, and outraged, began cursing God, and shaking his fist toward heaven. He hurled every foul and bitter insult that came to his tortured mind, blaming God for shattering his dreams and taking the pride of his life.

There's absolutely no way to describe the oppression felt in that house on that day. It engulfed us like a shroud. The family kept trying to console my uncle, urging him not to talk like that, but his grief brought forth what was really in his heart, and it was *not* pretty.

All I wanted to do was get out of there. It wouldn't have surprised me if a bolt of lightning had shot from the sky and consumed my uncle for his blasphemy.

If he ever repented and gave his heart to God, it is unknown to the rest of the family. He died from alcohol abuse, a broken, bitter, old man. But not before his bitterness destroyed his remaining son. He was handsome and outgoing, but his father's consuming grief over the loss of B.J. convinced him that his own life meant nothing. He just did not measure up; therefore he tragically ended his life while in his late twenties.

This distant uncle of mine is the only person that I ever saw so blatantly accuse and berate the Lord in that manner. But today I am convinced that there are many others who are holding grudges in their hearts and blaming the Lord for all of their hardships and misfortune. I'm afraid that some of those embittered folk can even be found occupying church pews on Sunday mornings.

Prayer:
Lord, help me be strong like Sister Molly when I am faced with the unexpected blows of life. Help me to guard my heart from bitterness when I'm broken and in pain. Most of all, Heavenly Father, help me say like Jesus our Savior, "Not my will but thine be done," when I don't understand some of the things that transpire in my life. In Jesus name I pray. Amen.

Chapter Sixteen

The Empty Nest

The Empty Nest

It was like stepping back in time when I opened the door of the closet. It was one that I seldom used because it could be accessed only from the boys' bedroom and it wasn't easy to get to. When we built our house, this closet was more or less an after thought because it was under part of the staircase that led to the attic. About the only thing it was good for was storage, and I forgot about it most of the time.

Today my mind was on the arrival of our longtime friend, Brother George Guy, a minister from Louisiana. He was coming the following morning, and the guest room needed some attention. Our boys were married and gone, and I had taken their bedroom for guests.

I went in, stripped the bed, and began vacuuming the floor. As I did, it dawned on me just how bare the room was. At one time it had *two* bedroom suits in it. I had bought both boys a lovely oak bed with matching dresser and night stand, and had told them that when they married and moved out, they could take their furniture with them. And they did.

Now, as I looked around, I realized how sparsely I had furnished the room after they left. My mind came alive with creative ideas on how to make it look better. I was immersed in happy plans for the future when I reached for the door knob of that closet and stepped into the past. What I saw caught me off-guard. Everything was just as the boys had left it. Nothing had been touched. Trent's old Reagan For President sign, that he proudly displayed in our yard during the election, was leaning against the wall, upside down. To one side of the closet was a rack of clothes that they had outgrown. Two nice leather jackets, three suits, jeans, and a dozen or so shirts were hanging there.

Sitting in the floor were two antique clocks that Joey had bought at the flea market. The clocks never worked, and Trent and Candy teased him about them so much, they wound up tucked away in the closet.

I reached down and picked up a small brown paper sack and peeked inside. There, neatly wrapped in tissue, was an old pendulum and keys to the clocks - just as they were the day that Joey had stored them. As I laid the sack down, I spied an old guitar capo and a small can of spray lubricant that Trent used to clean his bass guitar. Needless to say, my mood began to change. Closing the door to the closet, I continued to vacuum. When I pulled back the curtain to dust the window sill closest to where Trent's bed had been, my eyes fell upon the *final straw*. There lying in the window was a tiny, half used tube of Blistex. Anyone who knew Trent knew that Blistex was never far from his reach, because of his occasional fever blisters. At a point in time when this was his room, Trent had squeezed that tube, used part of the contents, then placed it on the window sill. It had been there ever since, just as he had left it. Stark realization set in as I turned aside, gathered up the sheets to be washed, and went downstairs to the utility room.

Before I could load them into the machine, the flood gates opened, releasing a gusher of tears. All I could think was, "That time will never be again! It's gone!" Gone were the rambunctious days that go along with raising teenaged boys. Gone was the excitement of them raiding the fridge for food to take camping on the big hill diagonally across from our house. Gone was the noisy chatter of busy life that came with the continual stream of buddies spending the night and sleeping all over their bedroom floor. A couple of those boys stayed so often   they claimed their own sleeping mat and bedding, and were even responsible for putting them down at night and taking them up in the morning.

I thought of Joey (Joel, Jr.) the oldest of our three children. Taller than his dad, brawny, happy, and sensitive to the feelings of others.

Trent, just 15 months younger than Joey, is aggressive, motivated, dashing, and always "chomping at the bit." Joey's gentle way with his siblings, his genuine affection for them and his "think before you speak" attitude had a calming effect on the younger two's impulsiveness. Joey ran interference for them and was constantly trying to keep them out of trouble. He was a fun-loving lad and could always find something to laugh about, especially when it came to his younger brother and sister.

I couldn't stop crying. The more I thought about them, the more I cried. Those happy-go-lucky, carefree days were past. My boys were no longer just mine. Their clean clothes, their meals, their well-being in general, didn't depend on me anymore. They now belonged to others.

I wasn't longing for things to return as they had been; that would be foolish. Those times could never be recalled. Our boys were grown men now. They had spread their wings and were finding their place in life just as their dad and I had done. Their moving on was a natural occurrence, and we were proud of them. But an era had passed and left me standing in a cloud of dust, and I couldn't help mourning its passing.

My Daddy Played The Guitar

Candy was coming down the stairs from her bedroom when her keen ears picked up the sound of my crying. Sticking her head in the utility room she had that, *"Who died?"* look on her face.

When I told her what had happened, we both started laughing. I had been silly to cry over such a natural thing as the boys leaving home. But almost in the same moment, the tears began to flow again. This went on for at least forty-five minutes. I'd stop, we'd laugh, then I would start crying again. Candy was such a comfort to me. At least I still had her at home. She and I loved to do things together.

Candy and Me

When Candy was younger, there had to be quite a bit of compromising on both our parts when we went shopping. During those early days, when we were at the mall, shopping for things that I was interested in, I would be just fine.

But as soon as we entered the "mod shops," where it seemed we spent most of our time, the music would be blaring. Then Candy would say, "Oh no, Mother's feet will start hurting." And she was right. I never could ignore blaring music. It had a way of grating on me, and before I realized it, I would be tired all over. My feet were usually the first to go!

Candy and I have been good for each other. She has stretched me by wanting to go with the latest fashions, and I've kept her in check with my old fashioned ideas of how I think Christian women should dress. It has been a winning combination.

Since we were in the public eye, on stage every week, I felt it important to look as good as we could. So when Candy was barely in her teens, she and I joined the spa and worked out every other day when we were in town. The spa where we were members staggered the days between the men and women. Ladies could go only every other day.

It was snowing steadily one morning when I looked out of my bedroom window. "Today is ladies' day at the spa," I thought. As I watched the snow come packing down, the thoughts of the warm sauna and hot tub, lured me from the comforts of my home. I grabbed my spa bag and away I went.

It was early and Candy wasn't stirring, so I decided to go without her. When I arrived, it surprised me to find only a handful of ladies in the locker room. I didn't notice that they were dressing to leave. I was in my own little world, rushing to get to the sauna to break a sweat. Just knowing that it was snowing outside made it more inviting.

Inside the sauna, there was a intercom hanging on the wall that usually played soothing music. I quickly stepped inside, stretched out my towel on the wooden bench, and laid down on top of it. I lay there for awhile, feeling warm and cozy when a voice came over the intercom. It was low and subtle. In fact it spoke several times before I realized that it might be talking to me, since I was the only person in the sauna. The voice said, almost in a whisper; *"go home .*
. . .go home . . . .home is where your heart is . . . .go home . . . ."

I raised up and looked around. Not only was I alone in the sauna, there was not another spa member to been seen. I was the only one there! Everyone had left because of the snow, and I was keeping the workers from locking up and going home too.

Embarrassed, I jumped up, ran to the locker room, changed clothes as fast as I could, and headed for the door. But before I could get there, a whole car load of ladies came walking in laughing and talking as they filed through the door. It made me feel bad that I had kept the workers from getting to close up and go home, but it also made me feel good to know that there were others that had the same idea as I. However I was too embarrassed to stay, so I went home and left it with them.

During that same era we also started going regularly to a beauty shop near the house. I'll never forget the day that Lora gave Candy and me our first manicure. Our fingers were so sore that evening that we could hardly do anything but giggle and moan about our sore "pingers." That was fun. We enjoyed wonderful times together. Then, it was as if I blinked my eyes, and Candy was gone too.

After Candy left home, it took me a long time to be able to go the mall by myself without having to swallow a lump in my throat. I was glad when the little "mod shop" that we frequented closed down and was replaced with something else. It was proof that nothing stays the same. Life moves on, and like a river it just keeps cutting new paths.

Joel and I were blessed that our children didn't venture too far from home when they left the nest. Neither of them moved to far away places like Timbuktu, or Kalamazoo. Candy and Kent even lived in the house next door for several years. The boys and their wives lived in close proximity too, and we were still traveling on our bus and singing together about three days a week. Our children's independence from their father and me has been gradual. It happened in degrees, and that has made it a little easier for me to let go.

Chapter Seventeen

Papaw and Mimi

Papaw and Mimi

"Would you like another crumpet Mimi?," Jasmine asked in her most proper, sophisticated, five-year-old voice. She and I were having a pretend tea party. Well it wasn't *all* pretend. We were sipping soda pop and munching cookie pieces from her tiny tea set in our den. Her blue eyes danced as she assumed the roll of an elegant lady in high fashion.

It was just an ordinary day. As far as I can remember, nothing of great importance was making headline news. But that picture is a snapshot captured fondly in the recesses of my heart. It was a cherished moment of shared pleasure between grandmother and grandchild. Jasmine is our first grandchild. Naturally all the events surrounding her birth were colossal to her grandfather and me. The day she was born her mother called us about six a.m. "Mom, I'm in the hospital. I've been here for about an hour."

"Candy, why didn't you call me sooner?," I asked excitedly.

"Well the doctor has me on *the drip* right now, and its going slowly. I'm doing fine so take your time about coming."

The hospital was just down the street from our house, and Joel and I arrived in record time. When we walked into Candy's room, I was amazed at what I saw. She was sitting up in the bed laughing and talking to her husband Kent and the nurses. Her make-up was applied to perfection, and she was in the process of drying her freshly painted nails. I couldn't believe my eyes! It was plain to see that she was having a ball. This was her moment and she was making the most of it.

My Daddy Played The Guitar

Now it had been a long time since I had given birth, and I was impressed with how things had changed in the past twenty-five years. Evidently they've learned something new, I thought.

But soon after our arrival *the drip* began to take effect. When Candy was hit with her first big contraction, she let out a scream. Before long there was another and another. During one of those moments she looked at me pitifully and cried out "Mama, I didn't know it would be like this!!" It broke my heart to see her suffer, but I saw that there are some things that never change.

There always has been a certain amount of blood, sweat, and tears in bringing babies into the world. It's God's way. He set that in motion with Mother Eve. With all of modern technology and things to help it along, childbirth has been pretty much the same all the way back to Genesis. There is only so much man can do without being detrimental to the process. It's like the little chicken, pecking his way out of the egg. Interference can bring death or debilitating injury. In most cases, nature has to take its course, and it eventually did with Candy. Before long, the pain was replaced with joy and celebration at the birth of a tiny, blue-eyed baby girl. When Joel and I finally left for home that day it felt like my heart was much bigger than it was before: that was the day Joel and I became Papaw and Mimi!

When our grandchildren came along I began to have certain days that I devoted just to them. We call it "Grand-baby Day." It's a time that they can all be together at our house and play, and many times spend the night. Joel hung a rope swing from a tall oak tree in the back yard that they've loved and enjoyed, and I usually serve their special foods: cubed steak, piles of steamed rice and butter, oven fried potatoes, and homemade biscuits.

As they got older Papaw taught them to ride the four-wheeler, girls and boys alike. He always makes sure before they come that it's fueled up, and supervises to see that they drive carefully and safely. Our creek is another big drawing card. They play in it for hours during the summer. It's a great swimming hole with an adjacent picnic shelter with table and chairs. Thankfully they all can swim, and Joel and I sometimes get into the water with them.

More Kodak Moments

I remember the day that Joey's daughter Taylor learned to dog-paddle and keep her head above the water. She was very young and had been playing in the water with Jasmine who is two years older than she and already swimming. When Taylor realized that her cousin was doing something that she couldn't do, she set her jaw with determination and spent the rest of the day learning to swim. Long after Jasmine left the water she continued - water logged and blue lipped, but having accomplished the task. That was the day that I learned that Taylor is not a quitter. She has tenacity and "stick-ability."

There are many "Kodak moments" that click into mind when I reflect on those times when the grandchildren were younger. One of those moments has to do with a pair of tiny silver booties that dangled from my car mirror. They were made from gum wrappers and given to me by an inmate at Ellis Unit #1 prison in Huntsville, Texas. I kept the booties there as a reminder of those men that we have ministered to, and from time to time I would say a prayer for them. All six of my grandchildren were fascinated by the little booties and knew where they came from.

One day Taylor's mom, Sue Ann, went to pick her up from school. Taylor, a third grader at that time, hopped into the car and nonchalantly began unwrapping a piece of chewing gum. Then she held up the foil wrapper. "Mom, Papaw knows a man that can make little shoes from these," she said matter of factly as she folded over a stick of Juicy Fruit and plopped it into her mouth. "Your Papaw knows a lot of unusual people" was Sue Ann's come back with a twinkle in her eye and one raised brow. "Yeah, and a lot of 'em are in jail!" was Taylor 's reply as the Juicy Fruit got juicier.

One day, Kent, our son-in-law, came into our house with Nicky who, at the time, was a three-year-old, energy packed, hunk of love.

"Mom," Kent said to me, "Nick has written a song for you." Then with a little coaxing, he began to sing with nostrils flaring: "I love you Mimi, I love you Mimi. You give us popsicles and candy. . . .I love you Mimi." When he finished, I gave him a big hug and truthfully said, "Nick *that* is the most beautiful song I have ever heard!"

Many of those memories that I cherish and hold dear are just special little moments - like the time five-year-old William was spending the day with us:

It was a warm spring afternoon and William was helping me pick up sticks in the front yard to burn. I was pre-occupied with cleaning the yard when he spoke up, "Mimi, let's sit down for a while and enjoy the fire." He had a far-away look in his eyes, just like Trent, his dad, did when he was little. He was so cute with that big shock of hair and dimples, and completely trusting and guileless. At that moment it pained me to think of him growing up and being thrust into a world that would challenge those lovable characteristics. Of course, that's what growing up is all about, and I was confident that he had what it took to see him through, but it didn't stop me from wishing that I could protect him from the inevitable. As the glowing embers crackled and popped and the sweet smell of wood smoke filled the air, grandmother and grandson sat with warm hearts, basking in the joy of each other's company.

It was in times like those that I reflected on Mama Rogers and Mama Goodman: how their godly values had become a lasting part of me by just being in their presence. Now I hoped that I could do the same for my grandchildren.

Joel and I have been blessed with our off-spring. We don't have to lie awake at night and worry and wonder if our grandchildren are being cared for. Thank the Lord their parents are together, loving each other, loving the Lord, and raising their children in Christian homes. This is a remarkable accomplishment in this day of broken relationships, and we are ever thankful to God for His mercies in this regard.

It thrills Joel and me that our grandchildren are interested in music. Jasmine is showing promise and is already pursuing a career in writing and singing. They all seem to have a natural inclination to play musical instruments as well. Madeleine Grace, William's older sister by three years, has become quite good on the piano. She is the studious one. This olive-skinned, dark-eyed beauty is an honor student and usually comes to the house with a library book in her hand. But when she sits down at the piano to play, the others follow suit. They gather around with the guitars and fill the house with music. These are times that bring much joy to mine and Papaw's hearts. But as they continue to grow older I'm aware that those special times are all too soon coming to a close. It could not have been more evident than when we attended Sarah's last dance recital.

Little Sarah is our youngest granddaughter, and so gifted and kind. She's the one that plays for hours with her cousins without a ripple of conflict. She and I have spent many pleasant days enjoying each other's company by curling up on the sofa in the den, laughing at *I Love Lucy* reruns and enjoying old *Doris Day* musicals.

When Sarah appeared on stage that day in her flowing ballet attire, it was plain to see that she was no longer the little girl I took her to be. She was tall, lithe, and looked like an adult. It took my breath away!

The hot tears came without warning and stung my cheeks. As I watched her dance and twirl, I knew that the driver's license, graduation, college, etc. were just around the corner and would soon replace our sweet times of togetherness, but so is life.

As I finish this chapter, the group that gathers for Grand-Baby Day is getting smaller and smaller. Each season seems to produce a new driver's license and with it, more outside interests. This is the way it should be. All of the caring, training, and instruction that they have received from their parents and us, has been preparation for their journey toward independence.

Our children and grandchildren are still a big part of our lives and the source of much joy to Joel and me. Yet the time comes for each of them to pursue their dreams and fulfill their own destiny. Thankfully Joel and I still have each other and our ministry, both still intact through all the changes that life has brought.

Prayer:

Father, you have blessed me beyond measure. Thank you for my children and grandchildren. You have kept all of us from danger and harm and I am grateful. And Father, I trust you to keep us for the remaining days ahead. In Jesus' name. Amen.

Chapter Eighteen

A Place To Pray

A Place To Pray

*I*t was 6 a.m. when I awoke. Everyone was still asleep, and nothing was stirring in the house. The minute my eyes popped opened I thought about the prayer that the Lord had answered for me and I whispered an excited "Thank you Lord."

The prayer was about something that looked impossible, but a need that was paramount in my life. I had spent a lot of time, energy, and emotion, on my knees entreating the Lord about this matter, and He came through for me! It was an absolute miracle and I knew it. As I lay there basking in the gentle glow of God's faithfulness, a faint but forceful command flashed through my mind like mental telepathy: it said, "*Dance!*"

My reaction was disbelief. I wondered where in the world *that* came from, and ignored it. Then I eased out of bed, made my way downstairs to the kitchen, and turned on the coffee pot. As soon as I had the first cup in my hand, I went to the den, sat down on the sofa, and again was overcome with thankfulness to the Lord.

"Father you heard me, and answered my prayer!" I said, looking toward heaven. Then the word came the second time: "*Dance!*" It was as clear and distinct as if someone had spoken in my ear, but it wasn't audible.

Then I realized that God the Father was telling me to make an outward show of my appreciation for the awesome thing that He had done. He wanted me to express joy by dancing before Him.

Now this was not a common practice for me; in fact it was very awkward. But I stood up, set aside my coffee cup, and kind of waltzed to the center of the room. Then with unbrushed hair, dressed

163

in robe and gown, I began twirling, dancing, and rejoicing before the Lord!

Sometimes it's easy to forget that we get our characteristics from God. He is the Father of all life, but man is the crowning glory of His creation. Only in us did He place a portion of Himself. The ability to love and hate, to know joy and sorrow, and the knowledge of good and evil.

I hadn't taken into consideration how my tears of sorrow must have grieved His big, compassionate heart. Now He was ready to see some happiness from me! This is very understandable. It is the same that any parent would expect from a child who had hounded and begged for something until he got it. An outward show of appreciation is expected to follow, along with an outpouring of love and gratitude.

That experience taught me that the Lord has feelings too. If I'm to have an intimate relationship with Him, I need to stay aware of that. Now when the Heavenly Father moves mountains in my behalf, I am quick to praise Him for it. Not just once, but many, many times. In fact I try to give Him "thanks" for an answered prayer, as many times, or more, than I prayed for it. It's a guarantee that He'll do it again, and again.

The Altar

Prayer is so important in the life of an overcoming Christian. It is also a great privilege. There is strength and refuge through an intimate relationship with God our Father, and the well that we draw from when we pray is always accessible and abundant. I believe that most Christians are aware of the power of prayer, but I'm not sure we understand just how to go about it. It is a learning process that I am still trying to perfect.

When I first became acquainted with the altar of prayer, I was just a child. Papa Rogers, my grandfather, found a wonderful, Spirit-filled church not far from where we lived, and he took my Aunt Joyce, my cousin June, and me to Sunday School. I was eight years old. The three of us became devoted regulars at that little church and I loved it. I loved the singing and the testimonies. I loved the way they raised their hands to worship. Just being in that atmosphere warmed my heart, and I could hardly wait from one service to the next.

I learned so much in the time that I spent attending that little assembly. The children's classes were great, and we were rewarded with our own Bible if we learned to quote scriptures, or say the books of the Bible. I eagerly participated and was rewarded, but the biggest reward is one that I still have today. That is the knowledge of the Bible and the experience of genuine, heartfelt worship. These things became part of my foundation, the basis of Christian growth that I'm still building on today.

All of the above has enriched my life in ways that are priceless, but I will have to say that the altar had the most profound effect. When I first saw people kneeling at the altar, praying, it had a strong impact on me, and I was never quite the same after that. From that time forward, when our pastor encouraged the church members to come to the altar and pray, I was among the first to go. There were two altar benches at the front of our church, in the space between the pulpit and the pews. One was for the men, the other for the women.

That's where I learned to pray. It was so rewarding, and nothing was strange about it. It was an accepted part of our worship, and most of our congregation, it seemed, spent time on their knees around the altar. There I could pray for my dad's salvation, or for my mother. It was a special place for me to talk to the Lord and just know that He was hearing me.

Sad to say, but today it is rare to find an altar bench in the churches where we minister. I have seen the elderly come to the front, kneeling without an altar, having a hard time getting down, and having to have help getting up, because provision had not been made for them to kneel and pray. I am thinking, *"Why? What is the reasoning behind removing the altars?"* By my own past experience, I realize that the church is about the only place that some people pray. If Christians aren't encouraged to kneel and pray at church, I'm afraid we, as a church, are sending the wrong signal - that personal prayer isn't essential. But it is essential!

Even in later years as a young Christian, it wasn't hard for me to cry out to the Lord when I was in trouble, but an on-going prayer life was not a part of my daily activities. That is something that developed along the way.

The Lord is so gracious and merciful. He never has forced Himself on me, but He's always been there when I called on Him, moving His hand in my affairs when I asked Him to. I think that some of the most hindering beliefs that got mixed up with my faith were the *fables* that I learned as a child - always expecting the instant fix or the magic of the wand. If what I prayed about didn't "poof" and get solved immediately, it had a negative effect on my faith and prayer life. What a deception. What a trick of the enemy. No one wants to *wait* on God, even though the scripture says:

> *"But they that* **wait** *upon the Lord shall renew their strength; they shall mount up with wings like eagles; they shall run, and not be weary; and they shall walk and not faint" (Isaiah 40:31).*

In this microwave society of instant gratification, we have all been affected. I have been just as impatient as anyone, becoming exasperated and discouraged when my prayers were not answered as soon as I prayed. But Jesus warned us:

"Ye do err, not knowing the scriptures, nor the power of God" (Matt. 22:29).

We must know the scriptures to understand that there is, most of the time, a waiting period to answered prayer. All we have to do is look at the lives of Joseph or Job - not to mention Abraham and Sarah or Hannah, to see that they had to wait. They had things to learn before their promise came. They had to walk it out. Their faith was tested to the bone. When my faith has been tested in this manner, I describe it as being peeled like an onion, a layer at a time. So many beliefs and false assumptions have had to be stripped from me . . . .in order to find the Lord on His terms . . . .and learn who He really is . . . .and just how much He cares.

In my continued walk with the Lord, I can look back, and see the prayers that He has answered for me. Some answers came almost overnight. Some took months, and some have taken almost the total sum of my Christian walk.

My Secret Place.

*"But thou, when thou prayest, enter into thy closet, and when thou hast shut the door, pray to thy Father which is in **secret**; and thy Father which seeth in **secret** shall reward thee openly"*
(Matt. 6:6).

My altar of prayer has had to change from place to place since those early days of my childhood, but to have a special place to pray is still very important to me.

When Joel and I pastored in Bastrop we had altars in our church and encouraged our congregation to frequent them. I remember pouring my heart out at that altar and shedding bitter tears the day that we told our congregation goodbye. But my most cherished altar was the one that I made in a small room behind the platform. It became one of the most important places of my Christian growth. Before church started, on most of our services nights, I went back there, knelt at a chair, and communed with the Lord. What I was seeking for was to pray in the Spirit. I had grown weary of having to spend most of my prayer time trying to press through to where I felt that I had come into His presence. I desired to enter into His presence at the very beginning of prayer, instead of struggling to find Him every time I got down to pray. There is a difference in just saying a prayer and really being in the spirit of prayer - that special place of communion with the Lord. Jesus said:

> *"Ask, and it shall be given you; seek and ye shall find; knock and it shall be opened unto you"*
> *(Matt. 7:7).*

I was asking, seeking, and knocking, and it did open to me. It didn't take long before the Lord granted my desire, and I found the entrance into His presence. It was through worship and praise! I found out that the Lord responds to sincere worship and adoration. He loves it! My prayer usually begins something like this:

> *Blessed be the name of the Lord, which is, which was, and which is to come. Father God of Abraham, Isaac, and Jacob, you are the true and living God, and there is no other. Thank you for allowing me to come into your presence. Not by my worthiness, but because I am washed in the blood of*

*the Lamb. Thank you Father for making provisions for us to enter your Holy of Holies, by giving Jesus, your dear son, willingly. It is through his torn body, which is the door to Your presence, that I come boldly to the throne of grace. Father, **you are love** and **in your presence is fullness of joy**. I declare your righteousness. I declare your holiness. You are perfect in all of Your ways, and Your ways are past finding out. Hallowed be thy name. Thank you Lord, that Your eye is upon the righteous, and Your ear is open to their cry. Thank you Father for hearing and answering prayer. You are my God and my Father, and I love you. Thank you for moving Your hand in my life when I ask you. You are a very present help in trouble. Hallowed be thy name.*

There are so many ways to exalt the name of the Lord in prayer. I love to brag on His creation at times and let Him know that I think He has done all things well. Like King David said, we (the human body, mind and spirit) are fearfully and wonderfully made. As is all of His creation.

Once I read a church marquee that said: *"Life is fragile, handle it with prayer."* No truer words have ever been spoken. As time goes by, and life becomes more complicated, we find ourselves in greater need of prayer.

Sometimes desperate situations call for desperate prayer. When I was facing my trying situation, I gravitated to the seclusion of my walk-in closet. There, I found I could spend more time alone in prayer, un-interrupted. That's when my prayers became more effective, and where many of them were answered . . . .the most important one being the prayer that God answered when I was told to dance. In that closet is where I began to have more exchange with the Lord. He would talk to me . . . .not audibly, but in other ways.

For instance, our group was experiencing a heavy work schedule. We had been thrust into the mainstream of the gospel music field. Our platform had grown to include large auditoriums, churches of all denominations, fairs. You name it, and we sang there.

It was a shock to the mind to see how God could take our talent, which seemed so little, and do so much with it. It was the loaves and fishes all over again.

Joel and I took our work and responsibility to the Lord seriously, the same as we had in our pastoral days. We knew that He had put us before all these people for His purpose, and we wanted to do it well.

The Vision (or dream)

With all of this in mind, during prayer one day, I asked the Lord how he wanted me to look. I am aware of my influence on other women, and that many will follow my lead, even without being aware of that fact. This is a position that I have never taken lightly. My conduct and my appearance in the public eye has continued to be a balancing act for me through the years. I'm always searching for the middle of the road. The word here is *moderation*: not too far in either direction, knowing that there is a ditch on both sides.

I am a Christian first, a woman of God. I am also the wife of a minister of the Gospel, and there are certain requirements that come with the territory, if we believe the Bible.

A Place To Pray

I want to *look* the part: not wearing my position like a badge, but in the same sense that a business woman needs to look like a business woman . . . .or a nurse needs to look like a nurse . . . .or more importantly, like the wife of our President, who as First Lady should set a good example and be ever aware of her role.

I have often marveled at some of our church mothers who seem to chaff under any restriction of dress. The reason often stated is that it doesn't matter how we look because "God is not interested in our outward appearance. It's what is in the heart that counts." My answer to that is "Try telling that to women and men who are running for public office - or to those who are trying to land a position with a large company!"

The higher the position, the greater the responsibility, like it or not. I have yet to see a First Lady with a punk hair cut, tight blue jeans, and extreme make up and jewelry. (I wish I could say the same about pastors' wives.) They know that it doesn't go with the office that they hold. The mother of a church, or a Christian woman in general, holds just as high an office, even higher. We are leaders - looked up to and emulated. What a responsibility!

This was the frame of mind that I was in as I was praying that day. God had given me an honored position, and I wanted Him to know that I was grateful. I wanted Him to be pleased in the way that I conducted myself. Mainly, I wanted the Lord to know that His will was most important to me. *"Lord, how do you want me to look?"* I asked. *"How can I please you better with my appearance?"*

These were not mere words. I wanted to know the answer, and I was dead serious. The reason for sharing this prayer is because it was answered that same day, and the answer was not necessarily one that I wanted to hear. It came as a complete surprise.

When I finished praying quite a lengthy prayer, I then lay down on the big pillow, there in the floor, closed my eyes, and more or less dozed off. What I saw in a dream or vision (I do not know which) made me bolt upright. It literally took my breath!

I saw a small snapshot of myself, but it was moving, and I was holding it in my hand. In the little picture, I watched as I took big, pink, rollers out of my shoulder lengthed hair, and it was *snow white!* In reality I had kept color on it for years. It was a warm shade of brown that looked very becoming, and I thought, very natural. This was to cover the small amount of grey that started showing up when I was still in my twenties. I had no idea just how white it had gotten, and when I saw this scene, I shot up from the floor, looked toward the ceiling and whispered hoarsely, "Lord, you don't mean it!" Then I thought of Joel. What would he say about this?

The next thing I said was, "Lord, Joel won't like this!" Then I knew that if I was going to put the Lord first, I would have to forget about how Joel (or anyone else) felt about it, and trust that He knew what was best for me. Then, in the same breath, I said, **"But that's okay. Lord, I'll do it!"**

I have never put color on my hair again. I didn't then, nor do I now, see this as a salvation issue. It has also never occurred to me that the Lord was saying that *everybody* needed to do the same. It was just an understanding between the Father and me. I asked Him how He would like for me to look, and He responded. He had done something special for me with the color of my hair, and He wanted me to see it.

When my hair started growing out, I was in for a pleasant surprise. It was white only around my face, to soften my appearance. The rest was a stylish, peppered gray, and Joel just loved it!

It looked as though I had spent a lot of time and money to have it done in that fashion. I've had women ask me, "Did you have your color done at the beauty salon?" I just smile and answer, "No, God did that." A few years later the Gaither Homecoming Videos became popular on TV, and Joel and I are regulars on them. Because of this, people stop us on the street or come up to our table in a restaurant to speak. I receive more comments and compliments on my hair than any other one thing. Over and over, folk tell me that they spot us on those videos by looking for my white hair and they love it.

If it sounds like I'm bragging, I guess you could say that I am. But I'm bragging on the Lord. He is awesome, and He has ways and means to bless us that have never entered our minds. And prayer is the key! It's wonderful to be able to go to God in prayer and have Him get involved in our day to day lives. James said in his little epistle; "...ye have not, because ye ask not...." (James 4:2).

Somewhere along the way, that scripture really got through to me. Now, I know that there is no need great or small that I cannot take to the Lord. If it's important to me, then it's important to Him. All I have to do is present it to Him in the proper manner, be persistent, and wait.

Selling Our House

When Joel and I decided to sell our home on Dickerson Road in Nashville, we knew it would take someone who needed this particular type of house to buy it. We had spent thirty-one years and raised our children there but the house had become too large for just the two of us, and we were ready to scale down. We had found thirty-two acres out in the country near a neighboring little town, and wanted to move there, and build a house more suited for us today - one without stairs!

My Daddy Played The Guitar

That wonderful colonial style home held a treasure of memories, but it no longer met mine and Joel's needs. It was time to move on, and our three children encouraged us to do so. They worried about the four lanes of heavy traffic that passed our driveway; there a steady stream of vehicles flowed, and it had become dangerous.

The move was going to be difficult. The first order of business was to sell our house. That was the only sensible thing to do. We had already bought the acreage to build on, but to go forward we needed to sell. Now Joel and I were really praying about this matter when our longtime friend and prayer partner, Brother George Guy called. Brother Guy, and his wife Sybil, were more like relatives than friends. The Lord uses him as a prophet at times, and he has spoken into our lives on many occasions.

Our house had been listed and on the market for six weeks without one call of interest. Our realtor was getting nervous and wanted Joel to consider lowering the price. The house was already listed at under the appraised value, and Joel was not inclined to drop it further.

He and I had been praying daily about the situation. We needed to move that piece of property in order to get out of debt. That's how things were going when the phone rang early one morning.

"Brother Joel, this is Brother Guy. I've been praying about the sale of your house, and the Lord has been talking to me. He told me that you will sell the house in seven days. This is Wednesday. That means by next Wednesday you will have a buyer."

Joel responded by saying, "My realtor thinks I should drop the price."

Brother Guy answered, "Don't come down on the price; just watch God work! And help me pray it through. I know what God

174

said, and oh yes, He said that the buyers are not from Nashville. They're coming a long way to buy your house."

Sure enough, in about four days another realtor came up our drive. I was standing outside when she arrived. She said, "I think I have someone who will buy this house. I know I don't have an appointment, but will it be all right if I call them to come and look?"

"Will it be all right!?" I thought, as she was talking. "Of course it will be all right," I said.

Within an hour those people came, loved what they saw, and agreed to buy our home. They were from the Bahamas. They needed a big house to start a Christian school in. We had to wait a few days for their financial backer to get in from London, England, to sign the papers.

When we called Brother Guy and told him that the house had sold, and how far they came to buy it, he said, "Well, that's far enough!"

Still Praying, Expecting and Believing

God is still answering my prayers. And sometimes He gives me a word in my sleep. Recently I awoke with a scripture resounding in my mind:

> *"The effectual, fervent prayer of a righteous man*
> *availeth much" (James 5:16).*

I needed that word. There is something that I've been praying about for almost three years, and at this point nothing has changed. The answer to this prayer is very important to me but I was becoming slack in bringing it before the Lord in my devotions. It wasn't doubt. I was just wanting to be careful and not weary the Lord with my request. I believe now that I was listening to the voice of discouragement. The apostle Paul said:

> *"Be anxious for nothing, but in everything, by prayer and supplication with thanksgiving, let your requests be made known unto God. And the peace of God, which passeth all understanding, shall keep your hearts and minds through Christ Jesus" (Philippians 4:6-7).*

When we come to God in the prescribed manner, humbly, thanking Him for all He is and all He has done on our behalf, then we can go forward with our appeal. We are encouraged by scripture to take our requests, our petitions, humbly and fervently to the highest authority, God our Father. If we are praying for something or someone that doesn't go against God's purpose, according to His will, **it will be granted**.

If our prayers are regarding a person or persons, we have to remember that God is gentle. He will not force anyone against his or her free will. But He has ways and means that have never entered our minds for turning hearts in the right direction, without force. He is the master of the heart! I believe that it honors God, and pleases Him, for us to ask for His help and guidance. It is a sign of faith on our part. Remember that Jesus said, *"Pray to thy Father which is in **secret**; and thy Father that seeth in **secret** . . . ."* King David also spoke of the "secret place."

> *"He that dwelleth in the **secret place** of the most High shall abide under the shadow of the Almighty" (Ps. 91:1).*

176

Prayer:

Heavenly Father, your timing is perfect because you see the whole picture. I know that you will come through for me; you always have. I trust you to meet my need, and Father I will try not to be impatient with you, because you have not been impatient with me. Thank you for peace in this matter, the peace that only you can give. In Jesus' name I pray. Amen.

Chapter Nineteen

Monuments

Monuments

*I*t was fall of 1983 when our plane touched down on the lovely island of Oahu. It was mine and Joel's first trip to Hawaii and I was excited and anxious to experience the grandeur of that Polynesian paradise. I had fallen in love with the place some three decades earlier by radio, never dreaming that I would actually get to go there. That was back in the 1950's.

In those days when Mother and the rest of the *Happy Goodmans* were away on a singing tour - at night, after Mama and Papa, and Bobby and Jimmy went to bed - I would lie awake and listen to the radio. It played softly by my bedside, allowing my young mind to drift gently to far and distant shores.

It was a cozy and secure set up. Mother being away, singing with her brothers and sisters for a week or two at a time, was normal for all. While "The Family" was touring, those of us who stayed at home slipped into a more commonplace routine.

It was early to bed, early to rise, school, homework, polishing shoes, pressing clothes, the normal things that fill a day, and bring on another. Since I shared the bedroom with Mother and her two sisters, it was quiet and still when they were away. But I didn't mind.

That's when I got caught up on my thinking and day dreaming. One of my favorite ways to do that was listen to the radio at night. My dial usually landed on orchestra music. It didn't interfere with my thoughts; in fact the sweet violins encouraged them. I thought about my future. And I wondered what lay in store for me. *What*

My Daddy Played The Guitar

kind of life will I have? Where is my husband? Who is he? Where will I live? Having spent only thirteen years on this planet, the anticipation of things to come was a glorious mystery to me. The one *sure* thing in my sometimes unstable existence, was God. He was my mainstay, my rock, and I determined that I could and would build my life around Him. Because of this resolve, I looked toward the future with great expectations. It could even be described as a feeling of *destiny*.

My heart was full of hopes, dreams, and total trust that life would be good, no matter who I shared it with or where it took place. I was convinced that my future was bright. The Lord was my dearest friend, my constant companion. I felt loved by Him and talked to Him in the still of the night. My plan was to have a Christian husband, and raise my children in church. Those were the thoughts that kept me occupied when I was alone and kept me smiling even when things weren't all that good.

As I lay there listening to the radio, ever so often I would catch a broadcast from Honolulu, Hawaii. The Hawaiian steel guitar would be playing in the background as the announcer painted brilliant word pictures that danced and swayed through my head. He said, "We are coming to you live from the beautiful *Royal Hawaiian Hotel* on *Waikiki Beach.*" As he spoke I knew for sure that I was listening to a program on the other side of the world!

Here I was in Wingo, Kentucky, snuggling 'neath the covers, trying to stay warm on a cold winter's night, and the announcer continued: "It's seventy-five degrees here on the lovely island of *Oahu.* I can see the waves splashing along the shores, tossing in the breeze, as we continue this program."

And I could see them too! I even *heard* them, whether in actuality or in my childish imagination. I could hear the breeze rippling and the waves sloshing along the sandy beaches of the Pacific Ocean, and I longed to be there.

Now thirty years later, here I was - with *my husband*, no less! It was a childish dream come true. Six couples of friends and relatives, including Joel and me, had decided to vacation together. I'm not sure who first came up with the idea of Hawaii, but I was happy about the decision. There were the Mayo's, Joel's sister Rita, and her husband James. Then James' sister Jo, and her husband, Harlan Nobles. Our friends, Huey and Libby Priest, were also with us. The eight of us flew to San Francisco and met up with our long time friends, Doug and Rita Hodges, and their relatives, Gayle and Tony Delmonico. We stayed overnight in California with Doug's sister Yevonne. Then she, along with the rest of us, made the short flight across the Pacific and landed in Honolulu. Doug and Rita were seasoned travelers and the experts. They lived only about five hours away from this beautiful place, had spent a lot of time on most of the main islands, and had wonderful things planned for us to do.

Right off we were greeted in the lobby of the airport by a group of young Hawaiians, dressed (just barely) in their native attire. They welcomed us warmly by placing gorgeous leis of fresh flowers around our necks. Then they began taking pictures - which could be purchased for a fee the next day. Of course all of us wanted the pictures; we certainly wanted to take mementos back home.

From the moment we stepped outside the airport we were awed by the beauty of the exotic plant life that greeted us. Our eyes just couldn't drink it all in.

Once we were settled into our motel rooms, according to Doug and Rita, one of the first things on the agenda was *Hilo Hatties*. If we were going to fit in on the island we must be dressed right. We had to go to her shirt factory right away and be outfitted with moo moos, flowered shirts, and thongs for our feet.

Everything about the tropics was different and we were eager to play the part of *Tommy Tourist*; flowered shirts, straw hats, cameras and all. After getting dressed properly, we could proceed further and see the sights. Some of the most fascinating places were the *Polynesian Culture Center* and the *Kodak Hula Show*. There they explained what was being said by the hands of the hula girls who danced and swayed to the music and the beat of the drums. We even went to a luau and ate roasted pig that had been cooking all day in a hole in the ground.

The whole trip was exciting and interesting, especially when we visited *Diamond Head*, the big crater left by an extinct volcano. Then on to the Dole Pineapple factory. One night we dined at sea, in a large catamaran boat, on scrumptious sea crustations. We spent the biggest part of one day visiting King Kamehameha's palace, one of the oldest places of residence on the island. We laughed a lot, ate a lot, took pictures, walked along the beach barefoot - went to the zoo, went to a gigantic flea market at the Aloha Stadium, bought souvenirs - but more than anything, we *oohed* and *aahed*. Everything was just so beautiful.

Pearl Harbor

However, there was one place that left us speechless. Pearl Harbor. It had been a U.S. Naval base on December 7, 1941, when the Japanese launched their attack on America. When we got there we found a beautiful marble monument erected to honor the 3300 service personnel that lost their lives that day. Many visitors from around the world, including Japanese, stood beside us quietly reading names. It was like a mortuary. Everyone spoke in hushed tones. We were standing on the site of an unspeakable loss to our country and the pain was still fresh. Among the four battleships lost during that siege was the *U.S.S. Arizona.* It is still there in plain view, just where it had gone down, with hundreds of our marines trapped inside. That ship sitting silently on the ocean floor, remains a watery grave to this day. It's an eerie feeling to watch the oil ooze to the surface in a continual weeping, causing it to look like the ship is still bleeding, after all of these years.

The military cemetery is located in what is known as the Punch Bowl, the concave area of an inactive volcano. At that awesome site there is an endless display of small white monuments - 28,000 to be exact - uniformly standing at attention. All of those scenes were very touching and stirred something deep inside me. It brought awareness of the price of my freedom to an all time high.

One evening after supper, some of our group suggested that we take off our shoes and walk along the beach in the moonlight. Rita Hodges, still playing tour guide, was always pointing out places of interest.

As we strolled along with the salt water breeze blowing through our hair, we were admiring all the luxurious high-rise hotels. Suddenly someone spotted one that stood out in the crowd. It was low and lovely - and *hot pink.* Rita said, "There's the Pink Lady! They call her the Pink Palace of the Pacific. Actually, she was the first plush hotel on the island and is recognized around the world as an icon of luxury." She went on, "If you stay there you'd better be ready to pay for it. That hotel is the ultimate."

My Daddy Played The Guitar

By now Rita had our interest aroused. We wanted a closer look and decided to go inside the lobby. One thing I had noticed about Hawaii: they are tourist friendly. Wherever we went, whatever we decided to do, we were welcome. Everyone treated us as very important customers. If not now, then later, was their philosophy. They know if you come back you may choose to do business with them, and tourism is their principal industry.

Finding An Old Friend

When we started up the walk leading from the beach to the back of the hotel, there was a sign bearing the official name of the Pink Lady. It read, *The Royal Hawaiian*. When I saw that, it stopped me dead in my tracks. The wheels in my head started turning so fast it's a wonder someone didn't hear them. "It just couldn't be the same hotel," I thought. Then I turned quickly around and of course there it was, Waikiki Beach, just as described on the radio, its gentle waves lapping along the sandy shores.

"There's just no way it could be," my mind kept telling me, as I slipped away from the crowd. Everyone else was examining the gift shops and the elegant decor of oriental rugs, furniture, etc. But I was in my own world, transfixed and moving around like I was sleep walking.

"If this is the place where that radio broadcast came from, I have to find out," I thought. "And if it came from here there's bound to be a room with windows overlooking the ocean." Then bingo! I found it when I stepped inside a large room on the left wing. It was an old banquet hall filled with memorabilia. It was a kind of museum with pictures hanging all along the walls, depicting the glory days of the radio broadcast that I had heard as a child in Wingo, Kentucky. The pictures boasted the call letters on the big microphones as well as the many guest singers, and of course hula girls in their colorful, flowered sarongs. I couldn't believe it!

Excitedly I went to find Joel. He had to see this. I felt like I had come across an old friend, and I wanted him to share the excitement. It had been thirty years since I had heard that radio program. Now here I was standing on the very spot where it took place.

It's a good thing that we were nearing the end of our vacation because the trip to *The Royal Hawaiian* was the high point for me. To think that the Lord let me *actually* go there, not just in my dreams, but with some of my dearest friends and the love of my life. It was just too much!

That night stands as a monument in my heart, more proof of God's awareness, and His unfailing love. When I need a "faith lift," I like to look at the small things - the seemingly insignificant things that wouldn't mean much to anyone else - to draw strength from. Those are the moments that speak loud and clear to me. It's as if the Father is saying, *I was with you when you thought you were alone. I was there all the time. I saw your dilemma, heard the desires of your heart. Now look what I have done for you! Just look where you are now!*

More Visits To Hawaii

Since that trip we've visited the Hawaiian Islands many times with other dear friends such as Jerry and Charlene Johnson. The four of us even found an active volcano on one isle that had covered the road and some houses. Ignoring the warning signs on the roadblock, we got out of our car and walked on the warm black crust all the way to where red hot lava was spilling into the ocean. There was a continual spray of steam from where the molten rock was meeting the water and solidifying. In the previous several months the volcano had added over two hundred acres to that particular island. Charlene and I got close enough to the lava to stick a stick in it and watch it disintegrate. That was a crazy thing to do, and I shudder when I think about it today. Maybe there are times that God "still winks at ignorance" because we came out of that experience without harm.

Recently we re-visited Hawaii with more dear friends, Pastor Dan and Sharon Gill. Interested to see the *Battleship Missouri*, known to many as the Mighty Mo, we went back to Pearl Harbor and stepped aboard history as we explored that gallant old warship. It was a moment to remember. When we got to the Surrender Deck, we stood where the signing of the Japanese surrender documents took place. That happened on September 2, 1945 while the ship set anchored in Tokyo Bay. Now since March 31, 1992 it stands watch over the fallen of Pearl Harbor. This battleship is called *Operation Remembrance*, a fitting symbol of our nations honor, strength and sacrifice.

Historical monuments are very important and necessary but each of us has our own monuments hidden in our hearts. One of mine that stands tall and that I visit from time to time is my first trip to Hawaii. It declares God's faithfulness to me.

My Favorite Scripture.
"Delight thyself also in the Lord; and he shall give thee the desires of thine heart" (Ps. 37:4).

Chapter Twenty

A Day In The Life Of A Gospel Singer

A Day In The Life Of A Gospel Singer

hen you travel extensively as we have for forty-plus years, to spread the Gospel in song, the experiences and mishaps are too numerous to recount. Some are funny, some exasperating, and many, just plain crazy. Here is one of those instances - a glimpse of what you sometimes have to go through to honor your commitment and make the date.

When Joel and I are in Texas for concert dates, we usually try to swing by Huntsville and sing at one of the eight prisons in that area. We even did a three-day revival in the Ellis Unit in 1998 where the crowds ran from six to eight hundred per night, and some one hundred men were saved.

Recently we were booked for an appearance at the Walls Unit on Saturday afternoon from 2:00 to 4:00 p.m. The Walls Unit is where the infamous Carla Faye Tucker was executed. It is so old that it once held Civil War prisoners.

We were on our way that morning at 6:00 a.m., when the almost-new engine in our tour bus shut down on a hill, fifteen miles from Palestine, Texas, right in the middle of the road! It was dusk outside and the day was just dawning, so our baritone singer, David Hall, grabbed a flashlight to wave traffic around us on the two lane road.

In a short time a nice young man came along and volunteered to tow our eighteen-ton bus over the hill to safety with his Chevy Dooley pickup.

We then called a mechanic who came thirty-five miles, and by 10:30 had us rolling again for the final ninety miles of our trip. We were relieved when we realized that we could still make our 2:00 p.m. appointment, but we had no time to lose and would have to go straight there.

Knowing that we couldn't go to the motel rooms we had reserved to shower and dress, we pulled over at a rest area about twelve miles from the prison to freshen up. Again the bus stalled and would go no further. Unable to reach the chaplain by phone, Joel, who just can't stand to miss an engagement, began to look for a ride for us and our equipment.

Finally a total stranger, also parked at the rest area, said he would take us to the prison in his pickup. Hurriedly, Joel and David threw our equipment in the back, I grabbed my train case with makeup and hair brush in it, and away we went. The man drove us to the prison door and left us on the sidewalk out front at 1:45. By 2:15 we had cleared inspection, and with the help of several trusties were set up and singing to the approximately two hundred fifty men who had gathered in the chapel. It was a powerful service and at the end, about twenty-five men raised their hands desiring to be saved and came forward for prayer.

But when the service was over we were still faced with the same problem of not having transportation. We had no way to leave the prison. Joel was taking it calmly but I was on the verge of panic.

I had already made up my mind to call our two sons, Joey and Trent, to send us one of their buses from Nashville when the chaplain spoke up and said he would take us back to our bus, or wherever we needed to go, but didn't have room for us *and* our sound equipment in his small Chevrolet. I was still thinking about calling my boys for help when we were ushered into the warden's office. After much deliberation, the warden told us that all of his *nice* vans were in use, but we could take the funeral van, if the chaplain could drive it and we could stand the ride. We eagerly accepted his offer but were dismayed when we saw it. It was a white maxi-van with bars over the windows that looked like it had seen *many* funerals.

David, Joel and I, along with all of our equipment, were soon loaded in the back section where there were no inside door handles, and from which there was no escape. The chaplain and his wife, who rode up front, were separated from us by more bars and plexiglass. From our place in the very back seat, Joel and I could not see the road ahead, nor could we see David because the headliner from the ceiling was hanging down in our faces. We rode this way for some 80 miserable miles to an airport in Bryan, Texas to rent another van for the rest of our dates, arriving just two minutes before the rental company closed at 8:00 p.m.

Meanwhile, our bus was being towed to a shop in Shreveport, Louisiana. Arriving at the airport on time required the chaplain to jump a few curbs and make a few sharp turns which added to the excitement. Please get a glimpse of this picture: I was wearing a black-and-white striped sweater (We had sung in our casual clothes because of the time factor) and was sitting in the back of this beat-up Texas State Correctional van.

When we stopped at red lights beside other vehicles on the four lane road, I could see the people staring at us pathetically and wondering what we were "*in*" for. I thought I had about seen it all up until then, but this was an altogether new experience for us, and it became hilariously funny. We began to laugh at everything. The further we went, the funnier it became, and we laughed until our sides hurt. What a trip. Surprisingly, we made all of our dates that week and it was worth it. It always is!

My Daddy Played The Guitar

The Abby

Another interesting event occurred when Joel, David Hall, and I were on a return trip home from a singing tour of the U.K. which included Scotland, Ireland, and England. We had toured with other gospel-singing friends for two weeks and had several hours between our connecting flights out of Heathrow airport in London. Some of us decided to ride the train downtown, look around, and have lunch. London is such an interesting city with its red, double-decker buses and the sirens from the bobbies that produce a sing-song melody on just two corresponding notes - not to mention the centuries- old architectural phenomenon such as the tower of Big Ben.

Joel and I had memories from the past that included St. Margaret's Church at Westminster Abby and wanted to see it again. We left the train and made our way down the busy sidewalk to the church. Standing in front of that grand, spiraled structure, we started laughing and telling the others about the time we had spent there, several years back on Easter Sunday.

It was during the time that our children traveled with us, and our family was invited to sing in London at the famous Wimbley Country Music Festival. Joel and I, along with our three teenaged children, flew over the Atlantic with a plane load of country singers that included Loretta Lynn, Porter Wagner, Marty Robbins and many others. They were going to sing their country songs, and we were going to sing the gospel.

We sang on Saturday. The next morning was Easter Sunday, and our family was looking for a place to go to church. We decided on the Abby. Joel hailed a cab and we arrived early enough to sit on the front row, directly in front of the pulpit.

A Day In The Life Of A Gospel Singer

The ornate podium stood several feet above us, jutting out from the wall in midair. We were surprised at how close we were to the priest when he delivered his sermon, fully dressed in his impressive robed attire. We were all suffering from jet lag (which makes you nauseous and a little disoriented). Trent, especially, was having problems with that, along with trying to keep his band members out of trouble, for which he felt responsible. It seems that some of them were being influenced by the lifestyles of some of the country band members. Trent was trying to keep these problems from the rest of us, and it had him weighted down.

I don't know if it was the heat in the building that morning (or the lack of it) that finished him off, but something did. Someone sitting in the pew behind us tapped Joel on the shoulder just in time for him to catch Trent before he slid out of his seat to land beneath the pulpit. He had passed out. When Trent passes out he becomes *ridged.* Joel and Joey grabbed him by each arm and he was as stiff as a board. They finally brought him around but had to keep holding onto him because he kept passing out, and every time he did, he got stiff and started sliding out of the pew, his feet heading straight for the podium.

We were glad that the service didn't last long that Sunday morning. We got out of there as soon as possible and took him back to the Kensington Hotel where we were staying which is next door to the royal family's Kensington Palace. Of course when Joel found out about the personnel problems that Trent was having, he stepped in and put a stop to that. Joel had a meeting with the band members that were giving us trouble and said to them, "Boys you are over here representing the gospel, and representing the Hemphills. If you do that in a respectable manner, we'll see that you get back home. But if you are representing yourselves and continue to do the things that you are doing, you are on your on and can get home the best way you can." It's not surprising that those boys straightened up, and Trent had no more problems with them for the rest of the tour.

Joel was telling David and our friends this hilarious story as we stood in front of the Abby that day. Then we strolled on down the street to look for a place to eat lunch.

I had lugged my purse for hours and was holding onto it for dear life. It had the entire sum of our product sales inside as well as my jewelry pouch with my wedding rings and a few more priceless treasures - with a value probably in excess of twenty thousand dollars.

Joel saw that I was weary with it and offered to carry it for a spell, and I gladly handed it over to him. When we got a couple of blocks down the street from the Abby, I discovered that Joel no longer had my purse! For a moment we just stood frozen in our tracks. Then pandemonium set in!

Where was the purse?! What had happened to it?! Then I thought about the long story Joel had been telling in front of the Abby, and we figured he must have set it down on the sidewalk while he was talking. As soon as we decided that, David Hall and Wes Newton took off running back to the scene. They ran across the busy street, dodging traffic, and made a mad dash back up the sidewalk. There were hordes of people along the streets but the boys kept zig-zagging in and out of the crowd at breakneck speed.

In a few minutes, we saw them coming back smiling and holding my purse in the air so we could see it. They said that when they got to where we had been, there were two elderly ladies standing there talking, and my purse was on the sidewalk between them close to the wrought iron fence.

At first David wasn't sure if the purse was mine or belonged to one of the ladies, but when he reached down to pick it up, they seemed not to notice. By that he felt sure that it wasn't theirs and brought it back to me. When he handed that purse to me and I examined the contents and found everything there, I did a little jig!

I didn't care what people might think. We had just had a miracle, and I was as happy about it as the lame man in the Bible who went jumping and leaping into the temple when he was healed!

We talked it over and supposed that the two little old ladies could have been angels in disguise. Whether they were or not we'll never know in this life, but I am sure that it was their presence that kept someone from making off with my purse that had our money, valuables, and even our plane tickets home in it!

Prayer:
Thank you Lord for your call in our lives. Thank you that you have always been there for us and made a way when it looked impossible.

Thank you Father for your traveling mercies that have kept us from harm in diverse situations. You are the true and living God. Besides you there is no other, and you have ways and means that we know not of. I bless you my Lord. I bless Your holiness, Your righteousness, Your faithfulness, and Your loving-kindness. In the precious name of Jesus our dear Savior. Amen.

Chapter Twenty-One

Israel

Israel

When we stepped inside our hotel room, the window curtains were blowing wildly and slapping against the wall.

We were bone tired. We had endured a flight of eleven-some hours, then a miserable one-hour bus ride from the Tel Aviv Airport to the Carmel hotel. By the time we got to our room nothing made sense. Especially those crazy curtains. Joel went over to the window for a closer look, and said excitedly, "Come here Honey." There, through the opened window, shining in the moonlight, was the Mediterranean Sea. What a sight! The foaming waves were splashing pleasantly on the shore, seven stories below. Evidently a maid had left our window open so that we would not miss this gorgeous view.

We were in Israel, and this was mine and Joel's first trip there. We had come with a large church group from Alexandria, Louisiana. Two bus loads to be exact. Charlene, my Bastrop friend, had called me and said that she and Jerry were going, and there was room for two more if we wanted to come along. We jumped at the chance, and here we were.

Our first day of sight-seeing was spent in Caesarea By The Sea (named after Caesar) where we saw the ruins of that great city. We visited the amphitheater that has been recovered and is now in use at times by school children for plays. We also saw the remains of the large coliseum that most probably had been used for sports events and exhibitions.

It was amazing to see all that the excavators had painstakingly dug from the sands of time there on the seashore. There was evidence of enormous racetracks with grandstands to one side. Much of the wall that separated the people from the track was still standing. Ancient art depicting scenes of skill and strength - deer, chariots, horses, and men in motion - had been painted on the walls and were still faintly visible. The paintings were being restored, one by one, to their original colors and brought to life again. One of the most interesting sites in that setting was the remains of Herod's palace. It overlooked what had been his grand swimming pool down on sea level, with stone steps leading to it. The pool had been ingeniously built so that the sea water could be let in and out as needed. I stood amazed! There was so much to see; it was hard to take it all in. Also uncovered were partial colorful floors of mosaic design that had once been the floors of public bath houses. There were outside urinals and stone commodes still standing. All of this was evidence of a thriving society of long ago - today, just a part of history.

We left there and went on to Cana where Jesus turned the water into wine, and to Mt. Carmel where the fire came down and consumed the sacrifice that had been soaked with twelve barrels of water.

At this awesome place, Elijah had ordered the death of the four hundred false prophets who were leading Israel into sin. The brook that is mentioned is still flowing, just over the crest of the mountain. Someone read the story from the Bible as we stood there that day. It was great! Then we drove to Nazareth and saw *Mary's Well*, still filled with water, and has been for over 2000 years.

We began the next day by walking to the seashore from the Jordan River Hotel. There we boarded a double-decker, sight-seeing boat that took us across the lovely Sea of Galilee. It was an emotional experience to realize that our Lord Jesus had walked those very shores, even tread upon the waters of that sea, and ministered in all of the surrounding areas. The Sea of Galilee is a fresh body of water, only seven miles wide and fifteen miles long. The day we were there it was as smooth as glass. It is a documented fact, however, that that docile body of water can go from calm to raging in just minutes. Fierce winds cut through the mountains, down the *Jordan Valley* and cause waves as high as the boat that we were traveling in. The leader of our group had the captain of the boat turn off the engine when we came to the middle of the sea. He then asked Joel and me to sing, and we sang, *Master of the Wind.* Joel also gave a short testimony of how Jesus not only spoke peace to the troubled sea, but how it was through Him that Joel found peace when he was prayed for and miraculously healed from cancer and depression.

Our trip to the Holy Land brought the Bible alive. Every day we boarded the buses for more miles, more sights, and more inspiration.

The Clock

In the front, left-hand corner of the bus in which we traveled daily, there was a big clock hanging for all to see. What I had noticed about the clock was that it measured time in military terms: instead of 1:00 p.m. (just after 12 noon) it read 13:00 and so on. This was a small, insignificant matter, and neither Joel nor I made mention of it. It was just there every day in plain view.

By the time our bus came to a stop at the hotel in Jerusalem, we were exhausted. I was happy to know that we would spend three glorious nights in one place. Up until now it had been one night here, one night there. (That's when I realized that I had brought entirely too much luggage!)

My Daddy Played The Guitar

The Jerusalem hotel *Shaloan* was luxurious and plush. We were all looking forward to a hot meal and then going to our rooms to crash. The meal was laid out in buffet style, and it was scrumptious. Joel and I ate, then excused ourselves to our room. After finally retrieving our luggage, we began to settle in for the night. As usual, Joel was lying in bed reading the newspaper while I was in the bathroom brushing my teeth. Suddenly, he said excitedly, "Honey, it's getting late! Let's hurry and turn out the light; it's *five after twenty!*" I nearly swallowed my toothpaste, I laughed so hard. When I finally caught my breath, I said, "I knew it was late, but I didn't know it was *that* late. It's later than it's *ever* been!"

The next three days in Jerusalem were power-packed. We went to the *Mount of Olives* and had a glorious service of praise and worship. Then we took a winding path down to *The Garden of Gethsemane* where the Lord Jesus prayed and sweat great drops of blood. It was easy to pray there; the presence of the Lord was strong. Some of those olive trees are said to be over 2000 years old. Just to know that they could have possibly witnessed Jesus praying before his crucifixion was very inspiring.

I called Dad from Jerusalem at 6 p.m. one day to let him share in the excitement. It was 10 a.m. in Birmingham, Alabama where he was. I let him know that we were praying for him and Lila from the Holy City. He loved that. I tried to make him feel like he was right there with us by recounting many of our experiences along the way. Joel was so good to talk to my dad from all of these faraway places, and he always said, "I love you Pop" before hanging up.

The following day we went to visit the *Western Wall*, known also as the *Wailing Wall*, inside the old city. It was an emotional experience to witness the constant praying of the Jews there. The

Western Wall is a part of the retaining wall of Herold's temple, located at the base of the *Temple Mount*. That ancient wall is a reminder of Israel's glory days and is known as their *most holy place*. That wall is as close as the Jewish people can get to pray where those two cherished temples stood because the *Temple Mount* is under Palestinian control.

We felt especially blessed to get to go up to the wall and pray with them. There were restrictions. The men aren't allowed inside the enclosure without wearing a *yamaaka*, the small cap that Jewish men wear on the back of their heads. The women are separated from the men by dividers and have a separate entrance to the wall.

After approaching the wall and having prayer, we had to leave by walking backwards. It is not allowable to turn your back on their holy site. We didn't mind; we were just happy to have the opportunity to experience their traditions and form of worship. While we were there we even got to witness three *Bar Mitzvah's*.

One of the most touching scenes that day was when a group of young Rabbis came dancing down the steps of a building where they study, and danced and sang all the way to the wall. It brought tears to my eyes. It's a moving sight that can be seen every week on certain days. We were blessed to be there on the right day.

"Armageddon?!"

At one point Jerry, Charlene, Joel and I, broke away from our group to go to the Dome of the Rock. That is the area above the Western Wall, occupied by the Palestinians. According to Muslim tradition it houses the rock on which Abraham offered *Ishmael*. (Their bible or *Koran* reads totally different from ours - our Bible states that Abraham offered Isaac). Anyway, this is the sight of one of the Muslims' most holy places. No one is allowed inside the

My Daddy Played The Guitar

Dome without first removing their shoes, then purchasing a ticket. Now Charlene is a very impulsive person, and most of the time this part of her nature brings a laugh. But on this day, it was no laughing matter when she ran up to the door of that Dome with her shoes on, just to peek inside. *She* knew that she wasn't going inside but the *guard* with the *rifle* didn't. He stepped in front of her, loudly demanding her to halt. Charlene stood her ground with him, toe to toe and eye to eye. She got in his face hollering just as loud as he was, saying that she wasn't about to go in, she was just *looking*. He didn't understand a word of what she was saying . . . .and he was bristling . . . .with his rifle held ready. At this point, I started backing off, trying to distance myself from her. If she was going to start an international uprising, I wanted no part of it.

Finally things cooled down, and surprisingly Charlene came out of it without a scratch. Actually the guard may be the one to be pitied. He had met his match. When we finally eased away, Jerry, always the soft-spoken southern gentlemen, smiled and whispered, "I was afraid that Charlene was about to start Armageddon."

Those are a few of our many experiences on our first trip to Israel. In less than a year, the opportunity presented itself for us to go back, and we did. Since then we have enjoyed many trips to the Holy Land. On several occasions, we have stayed in the home of our dear friends, Pastor Guy and Jean Garner. The Garners lived in the city of Ashdod known as the "land of giants" in the Bible. Sister Jean, standing barely five feet tall, has been dubbed by Joel as the biggest *little* giant that we know. Those trips with them were especially rewarding because Brother Guy had studied the lay of the land and was a great host and guide. He has since passed away and our loss is heaven's gain. But by staying with the Garners we had the chance to experience the Holy Land from a different point of view. It was absolutely great!

Joel and I have also guested in the home of Polly Grimes, who has a gorgeous house that sits upon a hill in Tiberius overlooking the entire Sea of Galilee. Polly, in conjunction with the Israeli Ministry of Tourism, made arrangements for us to go to the Golan Heights to sing for the Israeli Army. They also booked us to sing at a *kubutz* in Galilee, and at several large hospitals where victims of the terrorist bombings are treated.

We also sang at the Frank Sinatra Center at Hebrew University on the Mount of Olives, called today Mount Scopus.

These are some of our treasured memories of Israel, but probably the most harrowing experience happened the day the Garners took us sight-seeing in Jerusalem. There were eight of us all together: Candy and Jasmine, our daughter and granddaughter, along with our friends David and Michelle Hall, Jean and Guy Garner and Joel and me.

Stoned In Bethlehem

We had rented a maxi-van from Avis to travel in when Joel remembered that while in the City of Jerusalem, we were only five miles from Bethlehem. "Why don't we go see the birthplace of Jesus?" he suggested excitedly. But his excitement wasn't felt by the rest of us. We knew that Bethlehem was under Palestinian control. What we didn't know was, that because of the Intifada, no tourists were going there. But we relented and reluctantly agreed to go. I might add here that Palestinian and Israeli vehicles are distinguished from one another by the color of their license plates, green being the color of the Palestinians, yellow denoting the Israeli's. We had a yellow license plate, and that was a no-no. We looked like a van load of Jews. However, at the check point the Israeli guard waved us through. We made it to the edge of Bethlehem in the area of *Rachael's Tomb* when we found the main road to be barricaded. There, we had to go either right or left onto a smaller road. Shortly after turning right, we were surprised to find a group of angry Palestinian youths standing in the road with hands full of rocks waiting on us. Obviously, someone had called ahead and told them to get ready, some Jews were coming.

There was nothing for us to do but to step on the gas, and when we passed them, they began to chase us pelting our van with rocks. One large rock landed on top with a loud bang, and shook the van and us. By then our situation had become desperate. It was also becoming clear why those military jeeps and trucks that we had seen before passing the check-point, had protective steel mesh over their windshields and windows.

As we bumped hurriedly along in a cloud of dust, hanging on for dear life, and dodging every time we heard a rock hit, we began to wonder if we might be the next ones on the evening news! We were sure glad that we had prayed for protection that morning before leaving the Garner's home. God is faithful! Just in time, a man in a Mercedes saw what was happening and came roaring to our rescue. He rolled down his window and started shouting at the youths, "They are tourists, they are tourists!"

Then he motioned for us to follow him, and sped away with us close behind. He didn't stop until we entered a secured parking lot in downtown Bethlehem. In normal times this lot would have been filled, but today it was empty.

When the man got out of his car he introduced himself, and said that his brother was the Palestinian Minister of Tourism. He was embarrassed by our not-to-friendly welcome, and posted a guard to watch our van. Then he and his brother, who soon arrived, gave us a personal tour of the holy sights.

In the *Church of the Nativity*, he held hands with us as we formed a circle, and he asked us to sing. We all sang, *O' Come Let Us Adore Him*. Then the man led us out of Bethlehem by another way. After asking us to promise that we would come back, he smiled and waved as we drove off. Most probably we will go back since things have settled down, and tourists are returning there in great numbers. But there is one day that we will never forget as long as we live. That was the day we got stoned in Bethlehem!!!

Then there was the time we went to Egypt.

Chapter Twenty-Two

Me and A Camel Named Clyde

Me and A Camel Named Clyde

A brisk knock on the door of the motel room where Joel and I spent the night was our signal to dress for breakfast.

It was one a.m., and it seemed I had just closed my eyes. My pillow had left a lot to be desired and kept me awake much of the night. I made the remark to Joel that I now know how the cowboys must have felt when they used their saddles for pillows.

Oh well, this was *not* the U.S.A.; we were in Egypt, and today was a day of great adventure. We were about to climb Mt. Sinai. Our group had a goal to reach the top of the mountain in time to watch the sunrise. There was no time to waste. A bus would transport us to the base of the mountain at St. Catherines, an ancient monastery that dates back to 385 A.D.

From there we were to rent camels that would take us two thirds of the way up, then without their assistance we would climb for another hour to the mountain peak.

My decision to make such a grueling journey was carefully weighed against the odds. If the opportunity ever presented itself again, I would be at least another year older and not as agile as I am today. I chose to go with my husband and climb the mountain of Moses.

As our caravan of camels (carrying twenty friends from Nashville) began its ascent, I knew I had made a wise choice. The stars and the moon lit up a pristine sky. The Milky Way, directly overhead, seemed just beyond our finger tips.

In the darkness, from time to time I could see our silhouettes on the mountain side as we snaked along. Joel was on the lead camel and began to sing every old gospel hymn that came to mind, and we all joined in:

> *Out of Egypt I have traveled*
> *Through the darkness dreary*
> *Over hills and valleys*
> *And across the desert sand . . . .*

When we sang *Camping In Canaan*, time seemed to stand still.

Here we were on the same mountain, beneath the same stars, using the same type of travel as the Bedouin Nomads that have roamed the hillsides for thousands of years. And most of all, praising the same Almighty God. The God of Moses. As we slowly made our trek up the mountain I was moved to tears. It seemed that I could almost feel the breath of God in the early morning breeze that brushed against my cheeks.

That two-hour camel ride was an exhilarating experience, but after reaching a certain point, the camels could go no further and we had to proceed on foot. There were seven hundred crude steps now to climb before we reached the top. The steps were actually rocks placed by the monks from the monastery, through the centuries as acts of piety when they felt they needed to do penance. Some of the steps were loose, covered by pebbles and rock pieces that were likely to cause a trip or a fall, so every move had to be made with caution. The climb now became an endurance contest.

The air soon became thin, and ever so often, I just had to sit down and catch my breath. At that point I realized I was slowing Joel down, and neither of us might make it to the summit to see the sunrise. After coming this far I wanted at least one of us to have that

214

experience, so at my insistence, Joel waved goodbye to me and continued on. I stayed behind with a couple of likewise winded companions, and our Egyptian guide, Isom, to move at our own pace. Before long Joel faded out of sight. When I could no longer look up and see him, my need to reach the top of that mountain on time became paramount. It ceased to be something I *wanted* to do and became something I *had* to do. I had to be there with Joel and share the moment. This was a once-in-a-lifetime experience, and I couldn't afford to miss it.

Mustering every ounce of strength I had from within my almost depleted reservoir, I set my jaw with determination. I would make it to the top on time if it killed me. As I continued to climb without let up, my lungs felt like they would explode. My temples were pounding, and I felt nauseous but I steadily moved forward and upward.

Finally the outline of the precipice came into view, and there was Joel anxiously searching for me. When he spotted me he rushed down to help me with the remaining few steps. Tears were streaming down both our faces while we searched out the highest available boulder to rest upon as that awesome sight came into view.

The Sunrise

The shadows slowly began to fade and give way to a harmony of color that crescendoed into a full orchestra. The brilliance of God's glory disclosed itself with golden rays that swept across the horizon, creating an unbelievable sight of splendor and beauty that left us breathless.

Joel and I were at the pinnacle. There was no place to go from there but down. From where we were sitting we could look straight down for what seemed to be *miles*. We have had a lot of euphoric

My Daddy Played The Guitar

moments in our years together, been many places, and scaled some pretty high mountains, but this was the ultimate. And never had we put our physical endurance to a greater test than we would before that day was over, and it wasn't over yet.

When the thrill of the moment subsided by the light of the early morning sun, I began to survey my surroundings. It was then that I was reminded of the adage, *"What goes up must come down,"* and realized there was no easy way off that mountain.

The decision to take another route down was made by our leader and guide. This route was steps *all* the way, *thirty six hundred* of them to be exact. I'm talking about steps that sometimes had as much as a two foot drop. By the time Joel and I had tackled about a *thousand* of them my legs no longer felt like they belonged to me.

Just when I thought I could go no farther we came to a bend in the trail and discovered two little Bedouin boys leading camels. At this point the trail split and we could go back the way we came by camel or continue on foot down *twenty-six hundred* more steps. I felt I had just been smiled on.

"Oh Honey, get us a camel," I cried. Joel was hesitant, and I couldn't believe it! I was sure that those boys and their camels were there to save my life! Joel wasn't so sure but went ahead and rented two camels from Solomon, (two out of three of our camel jocks were named Solomon) for ten dollars a piece.

I gratefully climbed on board. However I wasn't on Clyde very long until I realized that there is a drastic difference between moving in an upward position on a camel, and going downward. In fact one has never lived until one has gone down a mountain on a camel. When I said earlier that traveling by camelback was the mode of travel used for thousands of years, I left out an important note. The wooden saddles, without a doubt, have not been improved upon in that length of time either. There are six-inch saddle horns in both front and back that gouge you in the stomach or in the back with each jolting downward step. I was constantly being thrown forward on that crazy thing, and later I had bruises to prove it.

I tried every conceivable way to make peace with that saddle - to no avail. Ever so often, when I could stand it no longer, I cried, "Stop! Stop!" Clyde would then have to get down on his knees in the gravel to let me off. To say that he wasn't excited about this is an understatement. It made him mad! He was mad at me, mad at Solomon, and mad at the stones he had to kneel on.

It was an undertaking to make him go down, and he fussed and fumed at every stop. He didn't want to do it, and wasn't going to unless he was forced. Solomon and the other boy were just children, about nine or ten years old, and were very sympathetic with me.

They made Clyde kneel down anyway so I could get off for a spell. I need to add here that ours were one hump dromedaries, with the saddle on top of the hump. Even with Clyde kneeling it was a long drop to the ground, and because of this, Joel just had to sit there and watch. He did take off one of his shirts and threw it to me for more padding, and I used my overshirt. Then I proceeded to climb back onto the torture rack. By this time I could hardly mount. My legs were like rubber; they just wouldn't obey the command.

Eventually I got one leg across Clyde's back, and found I could go no further. I couldn't get on, and I couldn't get off. The biggest boy saw my predicament and ran to the opposite side to assist by pulling me by the hand. When he realized that we were getting nowhere, he called the smaller boy to pull, while he rushed around and started boosting my backside with his shoulder. Before long I was on board again and was surprised to find little brown hands stuffing their own shirts in front and back of my saddle. Then we were off and lurching again. From that moment on I became resigned to my fate and started trying to get my mind off the pain.

Amused at the constant chatter of our young camel jocks as we moved along, Joel commented, "I can't understand a word they're saying." "Well, ever so often I hear the word sheesh," I countered. "I figure they are discussing the size of tip (buck-sheesh) they will receive for landing these two green horns safely at the bottom.

Those boys were proud of those ornery old camels. Every now and then Solomon would look up at me and grin, flashing his pearly whites against his sun parched skin. In broken English he would say, "Camel is good!" He wanted me to brag on Clyde. But in my ever-present misery I would groan in response, "Camel is *not* good! Camel is okay, but *not* good!"

When I was thoroughly convinced that I would not live to see the end of this experience, St. Catherines Monastery came into view. Clyde saw it too and broke into a full trot. (This response in horses is called barn-sour). He knew that the end was near, and he was as happy about that as I was.

My pain was greatly intensified with the pound of each hoof beat as Clyde galloped along. I glanced back at Joel who looked as though he was actually enjoying the ride. I couldn't believe it. He had either made peace with his saddle or was too numb to know the difference. As the margin between Joel and I continued to broaden, I yelled back at him, "Joel Hemphill, I have now followed you to the end of the earth, and this time I found the jumping off place!"

Well, we eventually got to the end of the camel ride, and I really did live to tell the tale. That night our group stayed at a lavish spa resort on the Dead Sea, and before the day was over I was lying in the lap of luxury enjoying an hour-long Swedish massage. As I was being pampered with another hour long foot massage and pedicure, little was left of the Mt. Sinai excursion except a few tell-tale bruises and the unforgettable memory of Solomon's command to Clyde echoing in my ears, Yaa-dee!!! Yaaa-deee!!!

Chapter Twenty-Three

God's Creatures Great and Small

God's Creatures Great and Small

*I*guanas began emerging from the woods around us, cautiously at first, then more aggressively once they got to the clearing. There were scores of them in all sizes and an assortment of colors. I was fascinated by the little pre-historic looking creatures. They were coming from the wild to be fed. Joel, David Hall and I were invited along to watch. We were in Honduras on the isle of *Roatan* and had come to sing and minister for a tent revival.

I knew this was going to be an interesting trip as soon as we left our American plane to board the little "puddle jumper" that was to take us to the island.

That realization hit me when I had to step around someone's big dog, lying at the entrance of the plane, and watched as cargo was being loaded inside with the passengers. Another clue was that we kept waiting on the air conditioner to come on once we were inside and the door was closed. It never did. I can truthfully say, that is the hottest I've ever been! I looked around at the other passengers and they were drenched with perspiration - so much so that they had given up on mopping it off, and it streamed down their faces. We weren't dressed for the occasion either. Joel and I both had dark dress clothes on, made of material that doesn't breathe, and I wasn't breathing too well myself. There wasn't a breeze of any kind stirring in that little hotbox. I thought I might pass out. But as the saying goes "All good things must come to an end" and eventually that memorable plane ride did.

My Daddy Played The Guitar

When the plane landed, our sponsor Dale Jackson met us at the airport. From there things began to pick up dramatically. We were escorted to his home for supper, a house that looked more like the Governor's mansion, complete with maids and attendants. His wife Jill had prepared a feast of broiled lobster tail, and they treated us royally.

The Jackson family is a wealthy and influential family on Roatan. Their ancestors who came from the southern United States in the 1800's, and settled the island, were descendants of a confederate solider who refused to surrender to the Union. A southern accent is still discernable in their speech, even among the Black Caribs who make up most of the present population. We were glad to find that there was no language barrier between us and also happy to find "old time religion" there.

Roatan was different for sure. But we found a sweet bunch of people there who loved the gospel in sermon and song. Because of that we had phenomenal crowds each night and wonderful spiritual services. Joel and I were surprised to find that our music had preceded us through radio by many years. They kept asking for songs that we recorded some twenty or thirty years back.

We stayed at Treasure Island, a resort whose owner was Dale's uncle. We were given the guest house and told it is the place where Charlton Heston, Julio Iglesias and other celebrities stay when they visit. It was a lovely bungalow with picture windows overlooking the Caribbean. The proprietor is a wealthy land owner whose seven-million-dollar mansion sits on a hillside above the lodge.

When we arrived at the resort, I kept seeing little brown, slick haired animals about the size of a small dog. They looked like nothing that I could identify from the States. They seemed oblivious to people and had the run of the place. To be honest those little creatures looked to me like overgrown rats with square facial features. When I pointed one out to Dale, he couldn't believe that I didn't know a *rabbit* when I saw one. Oh well.

Then one morning I was sitting on the veranda beneath the shade trees, admiring the emerald sea against a powder blue sky, and sipping on a cup of coffee. All of a sudden it sounded like rain drops splattering the leaves of the trees beside me. I jumped up to see where it was coming from, and found an extremely large, adult iguana, perched on a limb above me, relieving himself. That was my cue to go inside. We found out that the iguanas live in abundance all over the island. Dale had some friends, a man and his wife and children, who just loved those odd little reptilian creatures. That family took it upon themselves to feed the iguanas everyday at the same time in the same place and wondered if we would like to go along and watch.

We jumped at the chance. This is something you don't get to do everyday. Dale picked us up in his van. When we got to the appointed place, they had just finished unloading an assortment of fresh fruit - oranges, bananas, mangos, etc. in a pile close to a wooded area. Joel, Dale, David and I stood by and waited in quiet anticipation. Then those tropical lizards, God's little creatures, started appearing out of the thickets from several directions. Their desire for food had taken precedence over their fear of man. They came slowly at first, then picked up speed the closer they got to the food. It was captivating to watch. However my interest soon turned into alarm when many of them went right past the fruit and made a bee line for *me*! I started backing up and they kept coming. Then I panicked, turned and began running and shouting, "Why are they coming at me!?" I glanced over at Dale Jackson and he was bent over laughing so hard he could barely catch his breath. He yelled back, "It's your shoes!" "My shoes?" I questioned as I looked down at my bright yellow sandals. He continued, "They think your shoes are bananas!" I ran to the van to watch the rest of the feeding from behind closed doors. That was as close as I wanted to be to our scaly little friends. Joel, on the other hand held and petted a big one.

Now I don't view myself as a sissy. I bait my own hook when fishing (that seems to be the acid test) and even take the fish off the hook. I am an outdoors person and love animals, but there are a few lines that I draw, like having iguanas climbing around on my feet, or getting too close to the baboons in South Africa.

Baboons?!

When I read the note left on the table in our motel room I thought it was a prank. It read in bold print:

> **Please keep your doors and windows securely locked at all times. The baboons are a nuisance!**

"This has to be a joke" I said to Joel. We had just arrived at the lodge at *Kruger National Park*; it was broad daylight, and there were *no* baboons.

There was a busload of us gospel singers, and it had taken quite a while to get checked in and receive our six weeks' supply of malaria pills. While our host was taking care of those details, we had wandered around the place looking it over. None of us had seen any unusual wildlife at the time, and I doubt if anyone even *thought* of baboons. I hadn't.

When we were finally issued our key, and unlocked the door to our room, that note was one of the first things we saw. But I tossed it aside. It was getting late in the day and we had to unpack, bathe, and dress for supper.

The Lodge had prepared an open-air feast for us, and it was grand. We were entertained by a group of young African men, splendidly dressed in native regalia, who danced and sang in Swahili.

As they performed in front of the huge bonfire to the sound of tom toms, we feasted on wildebeest pie, ostrich, crocodile tail and who knows what else. I tried it all. I didn't go there to be squeamish. This was a once-in-a-lifetime trip, and I didn't want to miss a thing.

We and some other singers had come to South Africa for a two-week concert tour across this country by bus. When our plane let down in Cape Town we had just experienced the plane ride of our lives.

When I say *we,* I mean fellow gospel singers such as Stephen Hill, Larry Ford, Lorne and Jimmie Ruth Matthews, David Hall, Stan Whitmire, Ken Turner, and other regulars from the Gaither Homecoming videos.

Our plane flew out of New York City, for the exhausting trip to South Africa. This was a flight that I was not looking forward to.

Joel and I had been on enough of those big 747's to know what to expect. We usually wound up in the middle of a row of five seats, scrunched up for seemingly endless hours.

You can hardly move, and to get out of your seat and go to the restroom is an ordeal. You wait as long as you can because you have to disturb your neighbors by climbing over them. Those overseas trips give a whole new meaning to the word, "miserable."

Our tickets this time however, were purchased by our sponsors in South Africa. We were to fly Alitalia and were happy that they specified *business first class*. We knew this would mean a little more room, but weren't prepared for all that it included.

Once on board we were ushered into a very spacious area with padded, automatic recliners. When I say spacious, I mean each recliner had several feet all around it and could be automatically adjusted into a bed with the flick of a switch.

We were not accustomed to this kind of luxury when flying, and it kept getting better. The flight attendants assigned to our cabin were there for our every whim. When we ordered our meals we made our choices from a first-class menu, dined on white linen cloths with silver flatware, china and crystal! I was lounging back in my recliner sipping coffee from a china cup when Jimmie Ruth Matthews got my attention. She and Lorne were settled in to the left of us. She grinned real big and whispered, "LaBreeska, this trip is not going to be long enough!" I smiled and nodded in total agreement!

When our plane let down on the Western Cape, none of us were any worse for the wear. In fact we were all eyes and ready to go. We were amazed at how modern the cities were as we went from town to town and happy that the *Brits* had already been there. Because of them, English has come to be a second language, making communication easy. Our group was escorted by bus and had two great concerts in Cape Town. Then we flew to Johannesburg, and boarded the bus for more touring which included three days at *Kruger National Park*.

We also sang in Pretoria, Boksburg, Shiloh, and several other towns. It was a great time of seeing and learning the country, and we met many wonderful people along the way. The main disadvantage about being halfway around the world is the time factor. It is

especially difficult to make phone calls to the U.S.A. because you
have such a small window of opportunity when those at home aren't
in bed asleep. We usually made our calls late at night when I didn't
have sense enough to carry on a decent conversation. But I had to
call my daddy. I loved to surprise him with a call from far away
places and hear his reaction.

"Hi Dad. Guess where I am." I said.

"Sugar where are you calling from now?" he asked. I could hear
the excitement rising in his voice. When I said South Africa, he
hollered at Lila, "Nanny, Breeska's in South Africa!" Then I
proceeded to tell him the experiences we were having. Joel then got
on the phone, "Hi, Pop! We are sure seeing some sights and having
a great time."

I wanted Dad to share in the excitement and feel like he was
there. Not just in South Africa, but most everywhere I went out of
the country. With just a phone call, he got to travel right along with
us from the warmth of his living room while leaning back in his
well-worn Lazy Boy.

The following morning found Joel and me out on the open-air
veranda, a wooden deck that stretched from one end of the lodge to
the other. We were anxious to take in the view over a good cup of
coffee. The coffee pots were situated at intervals up and down the
walkway so that everyone could help themselves. When we went to
pour ourselves a cup, we were surprised to find that there was no
sugar at any of the coffee stands. When we pointed this out to a
waiter, he told us that they couldn't leave sugar lying around because
of the baboons; they would steal it. When he said that, it began to
settle in on us that they weren't joking! Then when we noticed that
the waiters carried sling shots in their hip pockets, we began to

examine the trees a little closer. Sure enough, there they were. The little scavengers were the same color as the bark on the trees and not easily spotted. But they were perched all around, watching for a crumb to fall or for someone to leave food on his plate. They were silent, wile, and sly.

At about 10:00 that same morning we were still out on the deck when we heard this horrific sound. Everyone started running as the sound continued to get louder and louder. We couldn't imagine what was going on since we had nothing to compare that awful racket to. Finally we stopped a waiter and asked what all the fuss was about. He said an elephant had broken through the fence, was in the swimming pool and couldn't get out. He was trapped and was ever more telling the news, disturbing the whole compound. With help he eventually got set free and headed for the bush in full gait.

Kruger was an adventurous stop on our trip to South Africa, especially when we took the bus ride through the park. We spotted lions lounging on boulders, giraffes grazing on treetops, elephants bugling and challenging us as we passed, and even a hippo trotting through the dry sage. It was great to see those lovely creatures in their natural habitat.

Touring South Africa was a positive, memorable experience. Joel and I wouldn't trade any of it. But I will have to say that our close encounters with the baboons made some lasting memories. We were told while we were there that a baboon got into someone's room and they tried to get him out by throwing rocks at him. The baboon just picked up the rocks and threw them back!

Then there was the lady who found one in her room, digging in her purse! After hearing those stories, I was happy that I had seen the baboons only in the trees; that was close enough for me!

Chapter Twenty-Four

Tea Time

Tea Time

One of our tours to the United Kingdom began in Fraserburgh, Scotland. We were there to take part in their first national Gospel Music Convention.

When we arrived, we found the climate, the landscape, and the people in that part of the world to be interestingly different from the U.S.A. Joel and I are always ready to make new friends and learn their varied customs. It was there that we discovered the importance of afternoon tea in European culture.

Since there weren't many hotel accommodations in the area, it was decided that we would stay in the home of one of our sponsors. By agreeing to this setup, Joel and I were breaking one of our long-time rules of not staying in people's homes.

As the kids of today say; "Been there, done that." However, our time spent in the home of Alex Duthie and his lovely wife, Nan, was very pleasant. They were accustomed to having house guests and were prepared for us. Our bedroom had a private bath and sitting area. We were pleasantly surprised to learn that Nan was a direct decedent of the famous 13th century knight, *Sir William Wallace* better known as *Braveheart*. She even named their daughter Margaret after his mother.

The Duthie's home is cozy and modest and is situated on the shores of the North Sea. From their well manicured yard one has a grand view of the imposing lighthouse and endless miles of restless sea.

When we are touring it isn't always easy to find a good private place to pray. Joel and I both enjoy spending time alone in prayer as

My Daddy Played The Guitar

well as praying together. So while we were there, he would bundle up daily against the relentless winds and take walks through the heather along the seashore to pray. Sometimes I would go with him, but most of the time I would seize that opportunity to be alone. We enjoyed the vast beauty of the sea and marveled at how resilient and adaptable you would have to be to survive such a harsh climate. The Duthie's and their friends would jokingly say, "We have three months of winter and nine months of bad weather." When we arrived there around the first of May, the farmers had just let the cows out of the barns that had been shut up for the winter. Ordinary cattle cannot survive those severe winters outdoors; only the long-haired Scottish ones are equipped by nature for such climate.

It is the same with the Scottish people. It seems that God has equipped them with a hale and hardy nature, a love for life, and an inner strength. Most of them were bi-lingual, speaking English fluently. But ever so often when we weren't engaged in conversation with them, they would talk to each other in a strange language. They had their own dialect. It was an ingenious concoction which seemed to be a mixture of Gaelic, Welsh and English. No one could make out what they were saying but themselves. They readily admitted that they had their own lingo and laughed about it often. They even tried to teach me a few phrases, but as soon as I left Scotland, *it* left me.

We were surprised to find how large a role music played in all of their lives. Every home, we were told (and found to be true) has either an organ or piano. During the bad weather those dear folk pass their time of confinement by gathering from house to house, singing hymns, and handed-down folk songs, and fellowshipping.

234

They love to sing and do so with gusto. Another thing that adds pleasure to their lives is "tea time." It occurs about mid-afternoon every day and is greatly looked forward to. While we were there they brought out mouth watering delicacies such as scones and sweet cakes, served with piping hot tea in the finest china.

David Hall stayed only a few houses down the road from us in the beautiful new home of Alex's daughter Margaret and her husband. Now, David, being an American, had not picked up on the importance of "tea time." Therefore each day when his hostess announced "tea" he declined because he doesn't care for it. It puzzled him at how dismayed they became each time he declined. He had no idea that his refusal was knocking his host and hostess out of a pleasurable event that they enjoyed every day. They were so gracious that they were not about to engage in "tea" if their honored guest refused. After a few days, David realized what was happening and he quickly agreed to "tea" the very next time it was offered. He was amused at how excited they became and started scurrying around preparing, rolling out the sweet breads and setting out the fine china. From then on he never declined "tea time."

While on this subject, I'd like to say that hot tea was served to everyone that came to our singings - from china cups, no less. This was amazing to me. It was strange to see the soft drinks, at every venue, stacked in cans on the counters of the refreshment rooms, served and enjoyed at room temperature. Ice is not an important part of their society. After spending time there I understood why. With their abundance of cold weather, they did not seem to need cold drinks. It was the same when we sang in Belfast, Northern Ireland. Tea time is a must and was served in the same manner at all the venues.

The Fishermen

One day Alex took us to the docks at Peterborough where the fishing boats were bringing in their catch. I never saw so many fish in my life. There were eighty different stalls of every kind of edible fish imaginable, flouncing around in big open barrels. It is a sight and a smell that one doesn't forget too soon: such a bounty of sea delectables provided by our great big wonderful God, just waiting to be harvested.

Of course, the harvest is accomplished by life threatening days, weeks, and even months out to sea. Many widows are left as proof of just how dangerous those trips are, and wives never take it for granted that their husbands will always return. This thought is an ever-present cloud that hangs over the heads of the families of the brave fishermen of Scotland.

We met many of the fishermen that day and found them to be a delight. Some of the first ones we encountered greeted us excitedly and called us by name! That was a shocker. They were friendly, with a boisterous happy nature, and were genuinely glad to see us. As soon as they spotted us they shouted out with that thick Scottish accent, "Joel and LaBreeska Hemphill, Condy's (Candy) parents!" Then we knew that they had been watching the Gaither Homecoming videos and because of that they recognized us on sight!

When the fishermen go out to sea for months at a time, it's in very modern, computer-operated fishing boats. For entertainment in their leisure time, they listen to gospel music and watch religious videos.

It was wonderful and surprising to find that those fishermen with seemingly tough exteriors were Christians! They told us how it came about. They said that several decades earlier when some had visited the *Faero Islands,* they found revival there and a Holy Spirit outpouring. Those men got saved and returned with their new found joy and helped to spark revival fires in Scotland. The results are still evident today.

We visited many places of interest in Scotland with Mr. Duthie as our willing and eager tour guide. He pointed out where several clans reside, calling them by name, and then took us to the ruins of an ancient castle not far from where he lived. What was left of that old castle was monstrous and spread out over several acres of flat land. Then at the back of the acreage there was a steep drop - off, a cliff that plunged into the restless foamy sea. It was a desolate and grim place with strong winds whistling through the grotesque remains. When Alex told us that this was where the *Dracula* novel was birthed in 1897, I shivered all the more. I was already cold, but that knowledge chilled me to the bone. All of those sights made me anxious to get back to the Duthie's home and to more cheerful surroundings, which included a sweet cake and a good cup of piping hot tea!

Chapter Twenty-Five

The Autobahn

The Autobahn

When we walked up to Vienna's *Heldenplatz*, (Hero's Square) there was snow on the ground. Children, and adults alike, were gleefully ice skating in an open air arena, fenced off solely for that purpose. Their playful laughter warmed my heart as we shivered in the cold. The four of us, Brother Carey, Jenny, Joel and I made our way to the blazing open-air fire pots and huddled around them, bundled, scarfed, and gloved, but still cold.

Pastor Carey Clark and his wife Jenny had brought us on a sight-seeing excursion. Our work was done. All of our church services and concerts were behind. Now it was time to see some of the country before heading back to the Sates. It was a given that we had to go to historical Vienna, Austria to see where Mozart was born, and here we were.

Two weeks prior, at the Clark's invitation, Joel and I had flown into Frankfort, Germany then on to Mespelbrunn for a time of ministry. Brother Carey had lined up several concerts and teaching seminars for us, not only in Germany, but in Austria as well.

We had some wonderful services and met some of the finest Christians that we have ever come in contact with. From our office we had sent the words of the songs that we would be singing, to be translated into German. That was a big help. As we sang, the words were displayed by projector on the wall. Because of this they understood exactly what we were singing about. It was very effective.

My Daddy Played The Guitar

Today the English language is a requirement in the schools there. But the older generation, even though many are bi-lingual, doesn't understand English. So we spoke and taught through an interpreter. We've done that on many occasions and it wasn't a problem for Joel and me.

What was a problem is when Joel tried to use humor, as he often does. He's always thrown in something funny when he's speaking, to relax our audience by getting them to laugh. When he tried doing that in Germany, it didn't work, and we couldn't understand why.

Come to find out, the saying "some can tell them, and some can't" really is true. Our interpreter just couldn't tell it right, getting the punch line in the wrong place. Therefore most of Joel's humorous stories just hung in the air, (or fell flat) leaving a big question mark on everyone's face. After several attempts, it then became funny to us, so all wasn't lost; *we* were the ones who had a good laugh!

Our sightseeing trip was by car on the expressway which is called the autobahn. Brother Clark, being our chauffeur, was behind the wheel. When we realized that we were clipping along at 100-plus miles per hour, mine and Joel's blood pressure began to rise. Brother Carey mostly kept the car in the center lane, continually passing the string of freight trucks to our right. But alarmingly, the cars on our left kept whizzing by us as though we were sitting still. Since there isn't a speed limit on the autobahn, which is Germany's and Austria's interstate system, vehicles go at a break-neck speed. Brother Carey was just trying to keep up and stay out of their way. I'll have to say he was doing a good job of it.

Because of the high fuel prices (diesel is $7.00 a gallon) you don't see big cars over there. Brother Cary's car was some type of

Volkswagen. Joel was strapped in the passenger seat up front, and Jenny and I were scrunched up and strapped in the back.

Sensing the danger that we were in, at one point I lamely asked Brother Carey, "Are you sure that you have good tires on this car?" He assured me that he did, but I was far from being convinced. After a while Joel had a question. (We were sandwiched in between several huge semi's and a string of Indy 500 racers, or so it seemed.) Hoping that everyone stayed in their own lanes and did what they were supposed to do, he asked, "Does anyone ever have a wreck out here?" Brother Carey's come back was accompanied by a knowing grin. "If they do they only have one." We knew he meant they probably wouldn't live to have another!

Vienna

We entered Vienna by crossing the Danube River bridge, found a parking place, and began to stroll around the town square. As we did, Strauss' famous *"Blue Danube Waltz"* came alive in my mind and filled my senses. I could almost hear the rise and fall of the violins in that lovely melody as we explored the city that day.

The town is the Capital of Austria and nestled at the edge of the Vienna Woods where the Danube River gently flows. The Alps, in the clouded distance add to its beauty and charm. Joel and I were awed by the designs and architectural styles that gave the buildings, some of which date back to the 12th century, a quaint 'gingerbread house' appearance. Those lovely old structures, the spiraled Cathedral of St. Stephens, the parliament buildings, the Burgtheatre, and Opera House looked like pictures on Christmas cards, snow and all! It is a place like I've never been and is absolutely beautiful.

Being a place of history, Vienna has a past, some parts of which they are not proud. On that same peaceful square, some 70 years ago, in 1938, thousands gathered to give Adolf Hitler an adoring welcome. The survivors of that memorable day lived to regret it, as some 80,000 Austrian citizens perished at the hand of the Nazi regime.

Dachau

While we were in that part of the world, Joel and I discreetly asked Pastor Carey to take us to a concentration camp. They took us to Dachau, the notorious Holocaust camp in Bavaria.

When we arrived we were pleased to find the prison open and on display for the world to see. I need to interject here that the Jewish Holocaust was one of the first history lessons that Joel relayed to me in full detail, soon after we were married.

But the very first was our nation's Civil War. I was aware of both, but they were passions of Joel's. We even spent our honeymoon in Vicksburg, Mississippi near the Battlefield Memorial Park. And while sitting on cannons left over from the war, Joel explained the battles fought there, calling the generals by name as if he knew them personally.

That war was a four-year blood bath that drenched our nation, with friend against friend, brother against brother, and is a blot that stains the pages of our young history. It also gives testimony to our disgraceful period of slavery that had to come to an end. So to speak of national stigmas, we all live in glass houses.

Having said that, it cannot, and is not meant to diminish the inhumane cruelties of the Holocaust. That was a time when an evil spirit seemed to come from the pits of hell, bringing with it untold misery, fear, and death. It was a blinding, merciless spirit, without feeling or pity, causing human beings to treat their fellowman in a way that they wouldn't treat an animal.

We saw the ovens, the bleak barracks, and the pictures of the emaciated skeletal living dead, and piles of human remains stacked like cordwood to feed the fires. The grounds and the walls of the buildings seemed to groan and cry out as we passed through them.

It was a heart wrenching journey that everyone needs to experience. We were glad to find that it is against the law in Germany to deny the Holocaust. While we were there, someone was just being released from a three - year prison term for that very thing.

Leaving that horrific scene, I wanted to be able to encourage every nation and its people to walk in God's forgiveness. We should not accept the burden of guilt for something that happened before our time, that we had nothing to do with. Even though the Trail of Tears, a heartless event in our past toward Native Americans occurred, there is not one thing we can do about it now. There has always been a lack of wisdom, judgement, and pity in high places that individuals such as you and I cannot control.

However, we need to know the past history of our nations so that through prayer and the ballot box we will do all that we can to keep such atrocities from being repeated. This is the power that God has given us as ordinary citizens. Unwarranted guilt and self-reproach are enemies of our souls, making us victims rather than victors.

Prayer:
Dear God, save your people from having to be subjected, ever again, to the horrors that we have just described. Thank you that you gave your dear Son, Jesus, to suffer in our stead and pay the ultimate price at the hands of the wicked. And I thank and praise the Lord Jesus Christ for being willing to die for my sins and the sins of the world. Amen.

My Daddy Played The Guitar

Whittenberg

Joel and Brother Carey talked it over and decided that our sight-seeing trip would not be complete without going to Wittenberg where Martin Luther nailed his 95 theses on the door of the Catholic Church. Those were his statements of doctrine condemning the errors of Catholicism. That very church became Protestant seven years later, and remains so today.

It's still standing and Luther's body is buried in the stone floor of the sanctuary. We went there and took pictures of the church, the pulpit, the door, etc. This is a part of church history that affects all Christians today, and Joel and Carey Clark were like kids in a candy store. They gave Jenny and me a refresher course on Martin Luther's courage to stand against the tsunami of hostile darkness in his day, and we all were inspired by it.

We were moved with respect for the man who brought light and hope to the church world after experiencing a personal revelation that the *"just shall live by faith."* His brave stand against the papal system cost him his reputation and high standing as a priest. Fearlessly, he spoke out against the common practice of buying indulgences which they thought purchased for them the right to sin. This revelation gave hope to the poor and brought joy to the hearts of the common people.

However, it isn't hard to see why not everyone received his message so well. Especially those who benefited from those practices. But he wouldn't keep quiet and he wouldn't recant. Martin Luther was then labeled a heretic and ran for his life. He stayed in hiding for the next five years. Then in 1522 he returned openly to Wittenberg and led the reformation. The rest is history. Thank God for his tenacity!

The Autobahn

Today citizens of Wittenberg, Germany are proud of their celebrity. Martin Luther is their claim to fame. He put them on the map, so to speak. The room where he taught reform to his pupils for endless hours, is still there as well as the desk where he penned many of his revolutionary writings. His home is also preserved, much as it was, and is open to the public.

Our visit to Luther's home town was very interesting to the four of us, but Joel and Brother Carey couldn't see or hear enough. They tirelessly went from building to building, but as the day wore on, Jenny and I chose to sit through some of the sights. To be honest, she and I became saturated with church history. Before we left, at mine and Jenny's suggestion, we found a great place to eat. After a hot meal, we went back to the little car, strapped ourselves in, and headed for the autobahn for a flying trip home.

Prayer:
*Thank you Father for those whom you have chosen through the centuries, to take a stand for the furtherance of the gospel. Have mercy on those of us who shrink back from opposition, **and** have mercy on the opposers. Bless us Lord with strength to endure so that "when the battle's over, **we too** shall wear a crown." In Jesus name I pray, Amen.*

Chapter Twenty-Six

Victory At Last

Victory At Last

Tapping lightly on the door, I quietly stepped inside. There, across the hospital room, lying on the bed, was an eighty-four-year-old man, faded and grey, his tall frame showing very little evidence of the handsome man it once held - like a flower of spring that had come and gone.

I was responding to my stepmother's call that had come just a few hours before: "Breeska honey, your dad has had a light stroke, and he is in the Methodist Hospital in North Birmingham. I think you had better come." With that Lila hung up and I made quick preparations for the three-and-one-half-hour drive south. Traveling alone in my car, I prayed and cried most of the way. *"Lord please don't take him yet. Give me another chance to talk to him. Help me know just what to say. I need wisdom and strength to say something to affect him and make him call on you for forgiveness and mercy. Heavenly Father I ask you one more time, please save my Daddy."*

It was hard to believe that I had prayed for this man for over fifty years. In fact, a couple of years back, I was ready to give up on him. It happened one evening when I was in my prayer closet, on my knees, thanking the Lord for His blessings. It had been a long day and I was tired. So when I got around to asking the Lord to save my dad, which had become more or less an habitual prayer of mine, it overwhelmed me. When I thought of how many times I had prayed this same prayer, the strength just left my body. Then I sat down on the floor and start crying and looking toward heaven and said, *"Lord this is not working. I've prayed for my daddy for over fifty years and*

My Daddy Played The Guitar

I see absolutely no change. I'm wasting my time on him. I need to be praying for someone else, someone who will respond to the gospel and the wooing of your spirit."

It was only a matter of days after that prayer when I learned that the doctor had ordered Dad to give up his alcohol and tobacco. He had been having problems with his equilibrium, and the doctor said his addictions were responsible. Somehow this encouraged me to keep praying. It was a change and one for the better. I know that God has no problem saving anyone with addictions. He is God. He can breath on anything that troubles us, or that has us bound, and it will fly away on the wings of His breath. Unfortunately, everyone doesn't know that. The enemy of our souls would love to make us believe that deliverance from addictions is impossible. And it is when we leave God out of the equation!

I really believe the Lord was intervening, and in answer to my prayers was using the doctor to take away any excuse Dad might have for not surrendering his heart to Him. For the next two years my dad had to learn how to live without those things that had been a part of his life since he was young. But giving up habits was not enough, you can be gun-barrel straight and still be empty.

Dad was alone when I entered his hospital room that day. I greeted him warmly and kissed him on the forehead, but I was determined not to let this opportunity pass. Time was slipping away! He was slipping away! "Dad," I began softly, with a tear spilling onto my cheek, "I need to talk to you. You are about to take a long journey and I don't see you getting ready. Ever since I can remember, if we were going on vacation or about to make a trip, you would spend days preparing. You would be packing, checking the car, getting things together. This is the greatest trip you'll ever make

252

Daddy, and I don't see you preparing to go." I could hardly get the words out, I was so overcome with emotion. He looked at me very soberly. He knew what I was saying and, for the first time, was willing to open up and talk about his spiritual condition.

He said, "Honey, I've been around Christians all my life, but it just never took on me."

"Dad," I answered choking back the tears, "this is the most important decision you'll ever make. You are facing eternity without God!"

The desperation of his predicament gave me the courage to say things to him that I had never felt free to say before, and he listened. He was released from the hospital that same day and I took him home. Dad immediately began to rally back and in a matter of days, regained his strength. In the meantime our son Joey, a very dedicated Christian, went to Birmingham to see his grandfather. When he left town I urged him not to miss any opportunity to witness to his Grandpa. "You'll find him very open," I said.

Late that evening Joey called and he was ecstatic. Mom, he said "You'll never have to worry about Grandpa's salvation again." He went on. "After I had visited with him and Nanny Lila for a while, I asked Grandpa to step out into the back yard with me. I told him that we had done a lot of things together but we had never prayed together. I also told him that he may have already given his heart to the Lord, but I wanted to hear him pray for myself. Then we prayed together and Grandpa gave his heart to God. Mama **he really got saved!**" Joey was rejoicing on the other end of the phone line, and I was rejoicing as well. Happy tears were flowing along with shouts of praise from Joel and me. This was a victorious end to my lifelong quest. *Daddy got saved!*

There was a change in the Rogers' household after that. Dad was happy in his new found salvation and even discussed it with his younger brother, Jimmy. Uncle Jimmy, a minister of the Gospel, had prayed for Dad for years as well. Dad even got strong enough to drive again and did great for the next six weeks. Then, without warning, that massive stroke came and ushered him into eternity.

Prayer of Thanks:

Thank you Father for your faithfulness! You have ways and means that we know not of, and your ways are as high above ours as the heavens are above the earth. You could have taken Dad with the massive stroke first, but you gave him a warning, along with a few days grace, to get his heart and house in order. God, you are awesome!!!

Dad's memorial service was very special. We could give him up a lot easier, knowing there would be a reunion one day. It touched my heart to see the friends gathered that he had made through the years. They loved and respected him for who he was and came one by one to share their stories with me.

There was so much good about my dad that makes me proud that I am bone of his bone and flesh of his flesh. Even though he and Mother divorced when I was very young, I always had access to him. I knew that I had a father, a provider, a caretaker. I never had to wonder who he was, where he was, or what he was like. He loved working in the yard, planting all kinds of shrubs, veggies, fruit trees and flowers. He was meticulous with his vehicles, washing them and changing oil at the precise time. He loved the simple things of life and would always take a back road, if he could, rather than the main highway. Many of those traits keep showing up in me at the most unexpected times - and make me smile.

Victory At Last

I never knew a time when my daddy didn't have a job, no matter how unimpressive it might have been - from a coal miner, to an insurance agent, to a police officer and patrolmen. His bills were never delinquent and he absolutely detested a liar. And even though his adjectives sometimes grieved me, I always knew that my daddy loved me and would do anything in the world for me. His favorite color to wear was brown, he looked dapper in a hat, and most memorable of all, *my Daddy played the guitar!*

For more inspirational material from Joel and LaBreeska Hemphill:

Books
CDs *(Music, Preaching and Teaching)*
DVDs

P.O. Box 656
Joelton, Tennessee 37080
Phone: 615/299-0848
Fax: 615/299-0849
Email: jhemphill@wildblue.net
www.thehemphills.com
www.trumpetcallbooks.com

"Partners In Emotion"
By LaBreeska Hemphill
Trumpet Call Books

"My Daddy Played The Guitar"
By LaBreeska Hemphill
Trumpet Call Books

"To God Be The Glory"
(Examining The Bible View Of God)
By Joel W. Hemphill
Trumpet Call Books

**"Should We Pray To God The Father
Or Our Savior Jesus?"**
(Biblical Keys To More Answered Prayers)
By Joel W. Hemphill
Trumpet Call Books

Books available from the above address or wherever fine books are sold.

LaVergne, TN USA
21 May 2010
183483LV00002B/2/P